History, Society and the Individual

Essays by John Morgan-Guy

Special Issue of
*The Journal of Religious History,
Literature and Culture*
2021

Volume 7 November 2021 Number 2
UNIVERSITY OF WALES PRESS
https://doi.org/10.16922/jrhlc.7.2

Editors
Professor William Gibson, Oxford Brookes University
Dr John Morgan-Guy, University of Wales Trinity Saint David

Assistant Editor
Dr Thomas W. Smith, Rugby School

Reviews Editor
Dr Nicky Tsougarakis, Edge Hill University

Editorial Advisory Board
Professor David Bebbington, Stirling University
Professor Stewart J. Brown, University of Edinburgh
Dr James J. Caudle, Yale University
Rt Revd Dr J. Wyn Evans, St Davids
Dr Robert G. Ingram, Ohio University, USA
Professor Geraint Jenkins, Aberystwyth University
Dr David Ceri Jones, Aberystwyth University
Dr Paul Kerry, Brigham Young University, USA
Dr Frances Knight, University of Nottingham
Dr Robert Pope, Westminster College, Cambridge
Professor Huw Pryce, Bangor University
Professor Kenneth E. Roxburgh, Samford University, USA
Dr Eryn M. White, Aberystwyth University
Rt Revd and Rt Hon. Lord Williams of Oystermouth,
Magdalene College, Cambridge
Professor Jonathan Wooding, University of Sydney, Australia

Editorial Contacts
wgibson@brookes.ac.uk
j.morgan-guy@uwtsd.ac.uk
TWS@rugbyschool.net
tsougarn@edgehill.ac.uk

Publishers and book reviewers with enquiries regarding reviews should contact the journal's reviews editor.

John Morgan-Guy
Portrait by his wife Valerie. Reproduced by permission.

The Owl of Minerva spreads its wings
only with the falling of the dusk.
(G. W. F. Hegel, 1820)

Preaching of Sermons is Speaking to a few of Mankind:
Printing of Books is Talking to the whole World.
(Daniel Defoe, 1704)

Never will we find the truth if we allow ourselves to be satisfied with what has already been discovered, as those who wrote before our time were not lords but guides. The truth is available to all men and it has not yet been fully discovered.
(Gilbert de Tournai, c.1260)

CONTENTS

Foreword	vii
List of Illustrations	ix
Preface	1
Two Clerical Dramatists and their forgotten heroines of the Celtic Revival: 'Ravishing' Evelina and Scorned Gwendoline	3
'Christian Sincerity': The Reverend Henry Handley Norris and Parochial Ministry	23
'The Country is on the Move': the Revds J. W. Walsh, F. H. W. Schmitz and the S.P.G. Mission to Emigrants from Liverpool	49
'The Biggest Stink in the World': Thomas Southwood Smith, Social Conscience and London	63
The Search for the Ideal Male: The Art of Hugh Easton	79
The Works of John Morgan-Guy	95

FOREWORD

This collection of essays by John Morgan-Guy was undertaken at my suggestion, on the grounds that being co-editor of this journal should not be a disqualification from publishing in it. The essays represent John's scholarly interests which have developed over fifty years of research and writing. They include medical, religious, social and art history. In each of these fields, John has made a distinguished contribution to scholarship. His work on medical history has reached from institutional histories to roles of key medical figures in the period from 1700–1900. His work on art history in Wales has been especially distinguished, John having been a major contributor to the Biblical Art in Wales project. In that role, as a fellow of the Centre for Advanced Celtic Studies in Aberystwyth, he contributed to the development of a new field in Welsh art history. It is, however, as a historian of religion that John is best known. His PhD thesis remains a seminal work on Welsh ecclesiastical history of the eighteenth century. As recently as May 2021, I attended two University of Oxford research seminars at which John's publications were cited with admiration. His work, with Roger L. Brown, in founding the *Journal of Welsh Ecclesiastical History* in 1983, established a journal that opened for research an aspect of Welsh history which had few publishing forums.

John's edition of *The Diocese of Llandaff in 1763*, published by the South Wales Record Society in 1991, is an enduring work which illuminates the diocese of Llandaff in the eighteenth century. Much of John's work has focused on the history of Cardiganshire and of Lampeter. His essays in the three volume *Cardiganshire County History*, in the 2015 history of St Davids diocese from 1485–2011 and his work on Lampeter's history published by the Roderic Bowen Library and Archive has been perhaps the most sustained and impressive corpus of work by a historian in the last half century.

John's work has been recognised by his election to fellowships of the Royal Society of Medicine, the Royal Historical Society and the Society of Antiquaries. It is fitting recognition of John's skill and range as a researcher and writer that this volume represents a further outstanding contribution to scholarship.

William Gibson, Oxford Brookes University
June 2021

LIST OF ILLUSTRATIONS

Cover: Hugh Easton, *The Risen and Ascended Christ*
East window of St Martin's Church, Roath, Cardiff.
Photograph courtesy of Martin Crampin. Copyright.

Frontispiece: John Morgan-Guy   iii
Portrait by his wife Valerie. Reproduced by permission.

Figure 1: Reginald Heber   3
Drawing reproduced by permission of the National
Library of Wales.

Figure 2: Henry Handley Norris   23
Portrait by Thomas Phillips, RA. Reproduced by courtesy of
the Rector of St John of Jerusalem Church, South Hackney.

Figure 3: St John of Jerusalem, South Hackney   36
Lithograph by the architect, E. C. Hakewill, 1845.
Reproduced by permission of the Rector of St John of Jerusalem,
South Hackney.

Figure 4: Thomas Southwood Smith   63
Portrait believed to be by his partner Margaret Gillies, in
the possession of his descendants. Reproduced by permission.

PREFACE

The five papers which constitute this issue of the *Journal of Religious History, Literature and Culture* have been selected from a corpus of material researched over the last quarter of century. The criteria employed in that selection has been twofold; that the papers have been unpublished hitherto, and that they represent areas of my interest in church history, medical history, and the visual arts. In revisiting these papers, it has proved necessary in most cases to update, and sometimes slightly expand, the original text.

'Two Clerical Dramatists and their forgotten heroines of the Celtic Revival: "Ravishing" Evelina and Scorned Gwendoline' was first written for a Conference on 'Women's Writing in Wales and the Celtic Fringe, c.1650–c.1800' held at University of Wales, Lampeter (as it then was; now University of Wales Trinity Saint David, Lampeter) in August 2001. I am grateful for the constructive comments of participants in that programme.

'The Search for the Ideal Male: The Art of Hugh Easton' was given as a paper at a Residential School for students on the University of Wales Trinity St David MA 'The Body Programme' – now, sadly, discontinued – on 27 May 2008. Again I am grateful for the questions and comments of participants.

'"The Country is on the Move": The Revds J. W. Walsh, F. H. W. Schmitz and the S.P.G. Mission to Emigrants from Liverpool' derives from research in the S.P.G. Archive, formerly at Rhodes House, Oxford, and now at the Weston Library of the Bodleian, which was undertaken in 2010 during residence at Oxford Brookes University as a Visiting Fellow at the Centre for Methodism and Church History. I am grateful for the hospitality of the Centre and in particular of its Director, Professor William Gibson, which greatly facilitated that research.

'"The Biggest Stink in the World": Thomas Southwood Smith, Social Conscience and London' began life as a lecture given to members of the Octavia Hill Society held at the Octavia Hill Birthplace Museum in Wisbech, Cambridgeshire, in December 2010. I very much appreciated the invitation to deliver this lecture to a Society of which I was a founding Vice-President.

Finally, '"Christian Sincerity": The Reverend Henry Handley Norris and Parochial Ministry' is once again the fruit of research in the Weston

Library of the Bodleian, and that of Pusey House, Oxford, undertaken during periods of residence at the Centre for Methodism and Church History at Oxford Brookes University. A second tenure of a Visiting Fellowship there in 2020 enabled me to complete work upon it.

It is my hope that readers of this journal will find within these papers at least something of interest.

John Morgan-Guy
Christmas 2020

TWO CLERICAL DRAMATISTS, AND THEIR FORGOTTEN HEROINES OF THE CELTIC REVIVAL: 'RAVISHING' EVELINA AND SCORNED GWENDOLEN

Figure 1: Reginald Heber.
Drawing reproduced by permission of the National Library of Wales.

I

That the 'Celtic Revival' in English literature began with the completion of Thomas Gray's *The Bard* in 1757 has become something of a truism. For example, Sam Smiles, in his *The Image of Antiquity*, says: 'However extensive antiquarian interest in Celtic society and culture may have been before the mid-eighteenth century, it is nonetheless true that the publication in 1757 of Thomas Gray's ode *The Bard* was one of the most important stimuli to a more widespread public understanding of archaic Britain and a begetter of that interest in all things Celtic now known as the Celtic Revival.'[1] The same point had been made two years earlier by the art historian Peter Lord, in his essay 'The Bard – Celticism and Visual Culture'.[2] In the context of antiquarian studies of Wales, the ode was to

https://doi.org/10.16922/jrhlc.7.2.1

provide inspiration for painters and sculptors, and the image of the bard become what Lord has called 'the logo of the age'.³

In fact, the story is rather more complex. Gray's ode had a long and intermittent gestation, and was not enthusiastically received on publication.⁴ Even if its reception was not as poor as that of David Hume's *Treatise on Human Nature* – which the author bewailed had fallen 'dead-born from the press' – it was certainly tepid. Arguably, it was not until after the publication of his friend William Mason's verse-drama *Caractacus* in 1759 that the reading public warmed to *The Bard*.

William Mason (1724–97) was a son of the parsonage; his father was vicar of Holy Trinity, Hull; and, after education at Hull Grammar School and St John's College, Cambridge, William was elected a Fellow of Pembroke College, taking Holy Orders in 1754. Far better known to posterity is his friend, Thomas Gray (1716–71), also a Fellow of Pembroke. By the time *The Bard* was published, both men were, in fact, recognised and established poets. Gray's output was relatively small, but sufficient in time to establish for him a reputation of being amongst the foremost of the English-language poets of his age. His 'Elegy Written in a Country Churchyard', first published in 1751, has retained its place among the masterpieces of English poetry ever since. Mason, too, had by the late 1750s a corpus of work behind him, including his 1747 poem 'Musaeus, a Monody on the Death of Mr Pope', and his verse-drama *Elfrida*, of 1752.

The two friends worked on their respective poems simultaneously. Mason was certainly researching his new verse-drama by 1756, and was encouraged, aided and abetted by Gray. In 1754 Mason became rector of Aston near Rotherham, which living he held for the rest of his life, and in 1756 he was collated to the prebend of Holme in York Minster. Thus after the mid-1750s he was mainly resident far from Cambridge, and much of his enduring friendship with Gray was conducted by letter. It was, therefore, in Yorkshire that the greater part of *Caractacus* was composed. As Edward Snyder said, 'Gray wrote letter after letter offering help (which was always accepted), making suggestions, and pointing out as tactfully as possible the absurdities into which Mason's ignorance so often led him.'⁵ This judgement is a little harsh, but certainly Mason's facile pen could outrun informed and considered thought. In July, 1756, for example, Gray had to gently remind him that Mona was Anglesey, and not the Isle of Man.⁶ Nonetheless, Snyder is probably right to suggest that Gray was actually more interested in Mason's

Caractacus than ever he was in his own *Bard*, and because of the way in which he freely shared the fruits of his own research with his friend, the verse-drama was an immediate success. 'The strange, wild beauty of the Druidical elements immediately caught the public eye and aroused great enthusiasm' –though their significance was wholly missed by the critics in the *Monthly Review* and the *Gentleman's Magazine*.[7] Two editions appeared in 1759, and others followed from 1762 to 1811.[8] It was Mason's *Caractacus*, 'the subject from Celtic history; the setting Celtic; [with] a distinctly Celtic atmosphere',[9] which really heralds the Celtic Revival in English literature.[10]

By 1759, when Mason's *Caractacus* appeared, the eponymous hero was already well on the way to being established in literary and artistic tradition as the epitome of nobility and patriotism. In the process, as Smiles has pointed out, he was all but reduced to 'a set of iconic co-ordinates' displaced from history.[11] The result was to be far from happy; nowhere is this better illustrated than in John Henry Foley's, albeit much later (1856), statue, Caractacus, now in the Mansion House, London, where, in Cosmo Monkhouse's words, barbarity is 'overcome by inward fire and outward beauty'.[12] However, Mason's depiction of Caractacus owes rather more to an earlier, perhaps less sympathetic and romantic vision. There is no doubting Caractacus' courage, his determination to resist the invasion of his land by the Romans at all costs, but, I would suggest, perhaps rather tongue-in-cheek, there is more of a conflation of Goscinny and Uderzo's Obelix and Vitalstatistix from their cartoon series *Asterix the Gaul* about him, than the icon of heroic patriotism who we find, for example, in Francis Hayman's 'The Noble Behaviour of Caractacus, before the Emperor Claudius' of 1751, the engraving of which Mason had almost certainly seen. Mason's Caractacus is the majestic, brave, hot-tempered old warrior chief (Vitalstatistix) who is always ready to drop everything and go off on a new adventure, especially if there is wild boar to eat and plenty of fighting (Obelix).

Mason looks back to the Jacobean dramas of John Fletcher, and in particular to *The Prophetess* and *Bonduca*.[13] Caractacus, as Caratach, is rather more prominent in the latter than the eponymous heroine. Despite Mason's biographer, John Draper's, assertion that he could 'find no trace of Beaumont and Fletcher' in his drama,[14] in *Bonduca* we are confronted with the same brave, impulsive warrior chief as we are in *Caractacus*. In Fletcher's play, Caratach is sceptical if not scornful of the prayers and offerings of the pacific druids:

> Cease your fearful prayers,
> Your whinings, and your tame petitions;
> The gods love courage arm'd with confidence,
> And prayers fit to pull them down; weak tears
> And troubled hearts, the dull twins of cold spirits,
> They sit and smile at.[15]

He would rather call on the war-god Andate,[16] *divine Andate, thou who hold'st the reigns / Of furious Battels, and disordred War*,[17] and rely upon the force of arms. We find a similar instinct in Mason's Caractacus, who, despite preparing to enter the pacific order of druids, is goaded still by 'the sharp, vindictive spear' of the warrior. The druids themselves perceive that 'gaunt Revenge, ensanguin'd Slaughter, mad Ambition' still cling to his soul, 'Eager to snatch thee back to their domain', as they tell him.[18] What Caractacus does not share with Caratach is what in today's vocabulary we might term the latter's strident male chauvinism. At a crucial point in the drama, Caratach rounds upon his cousin Bonduca (better known to us as Boudicca), accusing her of meddling in his battle-plan, and thus occasioning the loss of advantage and the fight. '*Home, / Home and spin, woman, spin, go spin, ye trifle*. . .' and, despairing, cries *O woman, scurvie woman, beastly woman*.'[19] Mason's Caractacus, by contrast, is heartbroken by the loss through capture – and, he fears, death – of his queen, his 'chaste . . . lov'd' Guideria, and is devoted to his daughter, Evelina.[20]

It is, perhaps, time to say something of the plot of Mason's *Caractacus* before examining the role played in the drama by Evelina. The setting is Mona – Anglesey – the sacred island of the druids, where Caractacus and his daughter have taken refuge after defeat by the Roman Praefect, Ostorius. Caractacus' queen, Guideria, was captured, and his son, Arviragus, he believes, fled the field. To Caractacus he is a coward, and, considering that his flight led to Guideria's capture, no better than a matricide. Caractacus sees no future for himself, and, tired and despondent, prepares to be admitted to the druidic order. To the Romans, however, he remains a potent threat whilst at liberty. Ostorius, having concluded a truce with Cartismandia, queen of the Brigantes (without Caractacus' knowledge) secures her two sons as hostages. They have the task of luring Caractacus from his sanctuary, on the pretext that Cartismandia needs his assistance, and that he will be reunited with his wife at her court. If they succeed, they will deliver him into the hands of Aulus Didius, the general sent with them with a sufficient force to effect the capture, and Caractacus will then be sent hostage to Rome and the emperor Claudius, thus removing once and for all the threat of resistance.[21]

The whole verse-drama is set on Mona, within the sacred grove of the druids, and within the span of a single night. Neither Mason nor Gray seem ever to have set foot on Anglesey; when, on 8th June, 1756 Gray wrote to Mason 'I see methinks (as I sit on Snowdon) some glimpse of Mona, and her haunted shades,'[22] what he 'saw' was in his mind's eye, for he was writing from his college rooms, and what he and Mason knew about Anglesey was largely drawn from Henry Rowlands's *Mona Antiqua Restaurata*, published in 1723 by the vicar of Llanidan. Rowlands was a native of Anglesey, and his parish was on the island. He had set himself to prove that Mona was the chief seat of the druids, what Smiles calls 'the heartland of the druidic order in Britain,'[23] and Rowlands gave an extensive account of druidic rites and the archaeological remains associated with them which were still to be seen there. Mason himself acknowledges his indebtedness to Rowlands' work, as well as to Edward Lhuyd's *Archaeologia Britannica* of 1707. Stuart Piggott's verdict is important here:

> The Druidic grove, unequivocally described in the classical sources, continued in general favour among antiquaries, artists, poets and the public, into the eighteenth century and beyond. In the eighteenth century its popularity was renewed. By the antiquaries, Druids were being transformed into the virtuous sages of ancient Britain, almost indistinguishable from Old Testament patriarchs and prophets, and even sometimes proleptically Christians;[24] among theologians, the deists were discovering that Natural Religion went back to the days of primitive man and was indeed as old as the world.[25]

The setting in the sacred grove is awe-inspiring. In his opening speech, the Roman general Aulus Didius, describes it – the sacred oak, the altar with a stream 'brawling' round its 'rugged' base, the 'wide circus, skirted with unhewn stone'; the backdrop of cliffs, with yawning caverns.[26] His hostages, Vellinus and Elidurus, the sons of Cartismandia, explain the scene to him. The Druid (one might almost be tempted to call him the Archdruid) and his brotherhood, the 'Sages skilled in Nature's lore', and the Bards, live in the caves. The 'wide circus' is the consecrated ground, the 'mighty piles of magic-planted rock ... rang'd in mystic order' wherein 'at times of holiest festival / the Druid leads his train'. Here, too, nightly, the bards, descending from their caves, 'robed in their flowing vests of innocent white', with their harps hymn 'immortal strains'. Aulus Didius, in his response confesses himself –twice– to be awed by the scene as so described.[27] The image of the white robed druid derives ultimately from Pliny. As Oliver Davies put it: 'Classical authors . . . saw the Celts as exotic and strange, bewitched by the often nomadic and nonurban character of Celtic societies in the early period, which contrasted with their own way of life founded on the *polis* and its more urbane values. Stoic influences can be felt, for instance, in the depiction of the druids as "natural philosophers", which we find in Strabo, and Pliny leaves us with a distinctly romantic and picturesque vignette of a white robed druid cutting mistletoe from a sacred oak with a golden sickle.'[28] Mason would have been familiar with these sources from his own reading.

Meanwhile, the druids enter the sacred grove, circle the ground in triple row, and asperge it. The preparations are made for the sacrifice of the milk-white steers which will accompany Caractacus' admission to the sacred order. It is at this point in the drama that Mason dwells on the pacific nature of the druids; they are, as Caractacus himself puts it, 'the sons of piety and peace', and they themselves proclaim:

> These holy groves
> Permit no exclamation 'gainst Heav'n's will
> To violate their echoes. Patience here,
> Her meek hands folded on her modest breast,
> In mute submission lifts th'adoring eye,
> Ev'n to the storm that wrecks her.[29]

It is quite clear that Caractacus sits uneasily to this understanding. His own thoughts remain dominated by the bitterness of defeat, of presumed betrayal, and by the desire for vengeance. In this he is contrasted with his daughter, Evelina, who shares his sorrow and his grief, but, like the spirit of 'the solemn shades' of the sacred grove wherein the action takes place, is the focus of quiet and virtue.[30] It is Evelina, in company with the chief druid, who dominates the action of the drama; each one of her speeches and interventions is crucial.

Mason may have been inspired by Aylett Sammes's engraving of a druid, from the *Britannia Antiqua Illustrata* of 1676, a work with which he was familiar, but in his calm, unquestionable authority his chief druid in *Caractacus* perhaps more closely resembles Zoroaster, as Mozart was later to depict him in *The Magic Flute*. On more than one occasion he rebukes the impetuous Caractacus, and reminds him 'I am a Druid, servant of the gods; / Such service is above such sovereignty . . .' as earthly kingship.[31] He and Evelina make a formidable pair.

Mason's Evelina is unswervingly loyal and virtuous; she is the epitome of purity. She has no illusions about the flaws in her father's character, describing him – accurately – as one of 'bold speech and warlike . . . rapt in high, heroic zeal' – that is, rash and impetuous.[32] Nonetheless, she stands by him, supporting him in his grief at the loss of Guideria, and, refusing to think ill of her brother, pleads his cause with her father.[33] As Caractacus, however unsuitable his candidacy, prepares to be admitted to the order of druids, so too does Evelina. The chorus of druids admiringly describe her as 'this prudent maid, / Now, while the ruddy flame of sparkling youth / Glows on her beauteous cheek . . .' preparing to quit the world, and vow herself to a life of virginal service,[34] as a member of the 'sober sisterhood' of 'sage daughters'.[35] Mason's words are laden here with what might be termed 'romantic pietism,' the pietism of a Count Zinzendorf, as J. Taylor Hamilton put it: which 'rested upon the conception of the grace of the Son of God, to which the believer owes personal fellowship with him and true sanctification and acceptance with God.'[36] This is not to imply that Mason was directly influenced by the Moravians in England – as had been John and Charles Wesley – but simply to say that it seems likely that he was at least sympathetic to a prevalent Protestant pietism of his time.

As an aside, it has to be said that Mason's evidence for the existence of female druids, as he advanced it, was somewhat slight, and his examples not altogether apposite or felicitous. In his end-notes, he refers to John Fletcher's play, mentioned earlier, *The Prophetess*, based on the story of the Emperor Diocletian.[37] Presumably the reference is to Delphia and her niece Drusilla. Although Diocles refers to Delphia as 'a holy Druid, / A woman noted for that faith, that piety, / Belov'd of Heaven',[38] his nephew Maximinian, to whom he is speaking, is more sceptical and scornful. To him she is rather one who 'sits farting at us, / And blowing out her Prophecies at both ends'[39] – a rather colourful way of dismissing her as a windbag. Certainly Delphia is portrayed more as a sorceress than a druid in Fletcher's play. Similarly, Mason's reference to Book XIV of Tacitus' *Annals* seems to put Evelina in uncomfortable company. Here Tacitus describes the overthrow of the sacred groves of Mona and the druids by

Paulinus Suetonius in AD 61. Among 'the enemy' were 'women, clothed in black, like the Furies, with their hair hanging down, and holding torches in their hands'.[40] These terrifying figures Mason in Caractacus incorporates into the ranks of the vassals of the druids, gathered to repulse the Romans. Here we find the black-clad sisterhood, 'with hair dishevell'd, and funereal brands / Hurled round with menacing fury'.[41] Anything less like this cross between the sorceress and the harpie than Mason's Evelina is hard to imagine.

She is not only pure, but shrewd. When Vellinus and Elidurus, the two sons of Cartismandua charged with luring Caractacus from his sanctuary, land on Mona, and present themselves to the druids, Evelina is suspicious of the veracity of their message. Acting true to form, Caractacus is taken in, and wishes to rush off immediately.[42] Evelina is not convinced, She has listened to the persuasive message of Vellinus, but has also observed the silence and troubled countenance of his brother. Here she notices that which the audience already knows, that there is an unresolved dispute between the brothers over their mission. For Vellinus, 'honour's voice commands / Thou should'st obey thy mother and thy queen' and be prepared to use any means of persuasion available, including lies and duplicity, to tempt Caractacus from Mona. For him, the end justifies the means, The betrayal and capture of Caractacus will redeem Cartismandua's pledge to Ostorius, and also, incidentally, preserve Mona from destruction. 'This our deed', he argues, 'has ev'ry honest sanction / Cool reason may demand'.[43]

Elidurus is not convinced, He sees their mission as a 'deed of baseness', the betrayal of the 'good old King, last of Britons, and Heav'n's own pledge', and does not believe that this action, however 'reasonable', will change Rome's 'deluging ambition'.[44] Yet honour forbids him disclose to anyone the duplicity of his brother. He therefore takes refuge in the silence which awakens Evelina's suspicions.

> Is it not strange, if, as the tale reports,
> My mother sojourns with this distant Queen,
> She should not send or to my sire, or me,
> Some fond remembrance of her love?[45]

She persuades the druids, and undertakes to question Elidurus, in an attempt to elicit the truth. Inevitably, Elidurus falls in love with her, and she with him, but he refuses to betray his brother, even at the risk of his own life. For he is to be put to the test, to the trial of the rocking stone. If what Vellinus has said is true, the great stone will rock at the slightest touch; if not, it will be unmoved. If the latter, then Elidurus' penalty will be death. The young man does not flinch,[46] even in response to Evelina's memorable plea: 'Truth and Secresy, / Though friends, are seldom necessary friends.'[47] Confronted with the choice between the betrayal of truth and the betrayal of his brother, Elidurus maintains his potentially fatal silence, even when, as a last resort, Evelina reveals something of her feelings.

> I am of royal blood, not wont to kneel;
> Yet will I kneel to thee. O save my father
> Save a distressful maiden from the force
> Of barbarous men. Be thou a brother to me,
> For mine, alas! Ah![48]

At which point, in the proverbial nick of time, her lost brother Arviragus, returns, thus saving Elidurus' life and honour.

On one further occasion is the action of Evelina of concern; Caractacus and his son are reconciled (the latter had not fled the field of battle in cowardice, but had withdrawn in an attempt to rally the faltering Britons),[49] Elidurus and Arviragus had joined in friendship, determined to fight the advancing Romans,[50] and Vellinus had shown himself in his true colours by fleeing to join with the invaders, thus exonerating Elidurus from any necessity to betray either truth or honour. However, it is the decree of the druids that Elidurus must die in his dishonoured brother's stead, and is released from that necessity only by the intervention of Evelina, who offers to die in his place if he is freed to fight 'for Mona'.[51]

The denouement is predictable; Caractacus, having slain Vellinus, is himself captured. Arviragus is mortally wounded, and dies in his sister's arms, whilst commending her to the care of Elidurus, who voluntarily agrees to accompany father and daughter into captivity in Rome.[52] The curtain comes down on an enigma; Caractacus embraces Elidurus as a son, in the place of the slain Arviragus. Elidurus is to be for Evelina a brother. However, in view of the mutual feelings of the two Mason has earlier hinted at, the question remains: what will their future relationship really be?[53]

What is not in question is the centrality in this verse-drama of the person of Evelina. Mason, as mentioned earlier, had in 1751 published an earlier play, *Elfrida*, which has an Anglo-Saxon rather than a 'Celtic' setting, in which the central character is a woman. Here again in *Caractacus* it is the sole female character, excluding the black-clad harpies, who predominates. Evelina is the true heroine, the epitome of loyalty and filial devotion, noble, beautiful, pure, honourable and self-sacrificing. She is no cipher. Her loyalty to Caractacus, her father, is not blind to his faults and failings. She is intelligent, determined, and courageous, prepared, if need be, to give up her own life for another.

It is likely that when he first composed *Caractacus* Mason did not envisage a stage performance of the drama. It was not, in fact, until 1776 that he prepared it for that.[54] The stage production was prefaced with a dedicatory sonnet, which included the lines 'Yet still our hearts in this great truth agree, / That Peace alone is bliss, and Virtue fame.'[55] There is no doubt that it is Evelina who most clearly exemplifies the grace of virtue in the drama. John Draper, using an expression from the epilogue to Rowe's *Jane Shore*, referred to Mason's earlier heroine in *Elfrida* as an example of female virtue in distress; it would not be inappropriate to see Evelina in the same light.[56] Mason's drama had an interesting after-life; the French librettist, Nicolas-Francois Guillard (1752–1814), and the composer Antonio Sacchini (1730–86) based their opera *Arvire et Evelina* upon it. Sacchini, in fact, died before completing the score, which was finished by Jean-Baptiste Rey (1734–1810), and the work was first performed at the Academie Royale de Musique (the Paris Opera) in April 1788. It is unlikely that Mason himself ever heard this work performed. Its first performance in England, with a translation of Guillard's libretto, and entitled *Evelina; or the Triumph of the English over the Romans*, took place in London in January, 1797, only three months before his death.[57] The translation was undertaken by Lorenzo Da Ponte (1749–1838), a Jewish convert to Christianity, who had been ordained to the Roman Catholic priesthood in 1773, but who is best known as the librettist for three of Mozart's most famous operas, *Don Giovanni*, *The Marriage of Figaro*, and *Cosi fan tutti*.[58]

II

In the year of Mason's death, the author of the second work which is considered in this paper, Reginald Heber, was fifteen years of age. His career as Oxford don, parish priest and missionary bishop still lay ahead of him. Edward Snyder said in 1923 'Attractive as a study of pioneers may be, it is through the study of a host of minor writers – followers, and often mere imitators – that one can come to estimate the interest taken by the general public.'[59] The truth of that is amply demonstrated in the 'Celtic Revival'; Snyder ended his study in 1800, but nonetheless contended that the eighteenth century was only a prelude to 'the brilliant era that followed.'[60] The stream that had its source in the eighteenth century broadened and merged into that of romanticism.

Reginald Heber (1783–1826) was, like Mason, a son of the parsonage. His father was rector of Hodnet and portioner-rector of Malpas in Cheshire. He was also a member of a Yorkshire gentry family, lords of the manor of Marton, but also of Hodnet itself, as well as being its parish priest. Reginald senior was a 'squarson'. Reginald junior was educated at Brasenose College, Oxford, where, as Michael Laird put it, 'he distinguished himself in 1803 by his recitation of *Palestine*, which marked his debut as a minor Romantic poet.'[61] The following year he was elected a Fellow of All Souls, and between then and October 1806, embarked with his friend John Thornton on what Laird called 'a somewhat unconventional grand tour'; most of mainland Europe being embroiled in the Napoleonic wars, it took them instead through Scandinavia, Russia, the Caucasus and the Crimea. These travels introduced him to Eastern Orthodox Christianity, and, through the Tartar community in Crimea, to Islam. On his return, he was ordained in 1807, and succeeded his father as rector and squire of Hodnet. He married in 1809 the daughter of William Shipley, Dean of St Asaph, necessitating the surrender of his Oxford Fellowship. (Later, in 1817, through the influence of his father-in-law, he became also a prebendary of St Asaph.) To these responsibilities were added the Bampton lectureship at Oxford (in 1815) and, in 1822, the Preachership at Lincoln's Inn. Heber was thus at once a conscientious parish priest, a respected theologian, and an intellectually gifted preacher.

In his day, he was also admired for his poetry, and today he still holds his place in the history of hymnody –'Holy, Holy, Holy, Lord God Almighty' being, perhaps, the most memorable of his compositions. It has to be conceded that as a poet he is now all but forgotten, and his work still awaits serious critical consideration. Certainly his place in the Celtic Revival has not been appreciated, and yet he was more closely bound to Wales than were either Thomas Gray or William Mason. As noted above, in 1809 at the age of 26, he had married Amelia, the youngest daughter of the Dean of St Asaph and Vicar of Wrexham, William Shipley, and until his departure for India in 1823 he was to divide his time between his Cheshire rectory and St Asaph. He was a frequent visitor also to Llangedwyn, the home of the MP Charles Watkins Williams Wynne, who, as President of the Board of Commissioners for the affairs of India, induced him to accept the bishopric of Calcutta, an offer which led to Heber's premature death in 1826.[62]

At Llangedwyn Hall Heber became enthralled by the music of the Welsh harp, and wrote several of his poems and hymns for Welsh airs and tunes. Of the hymns, that for vespertide, 'God who madest earth and heaven' was written for the tune 'Ar hyd y nos'. 'The rising of the sun' (a hunting song), 'The moon in silent brightness', and 'I mourn not the forest whose verdure is dying' were all written for singing to Welsh airs with harp accompaniment.[63] His premature death was widely lamented, in Wales as elsewhere, and brought forth at least one elegy in Welsh, by the Revd John Blackwell,[64] the last two verses of which are, in fact, a translation of Heber's own vesper hymn.[65]

The work of Heber discussed here is his unfinished verse-drama, *The Masque of Gwendolen*. Heber's widow, Amelia, printed the fragments of the masque in her massive, two-volume, life of her husband in 1830, and they were later reprinted in his *Miscellaneous Poems*.[66] Amelia Heber noted that the masque had been inspired by Geoffrey Chaucer's 'Wife of Bath's Tale',[67] but 'inspiration' is the word, for Heber departs radically from the text. What survives, as his widow observed, was that his plot turns on a solution to the same riddle as that propounded by Chaucer. Heber began work on his masque in 1816, but for some unspecified reason, it was laid aside and never completed.

The 'Wife of Bath's Tale' is among the most celebrated, and argued over, of Chaucer's *Canterbury Tales*. It has an Arthurian setting, abounds in magic, and, by some authors, has in recent years been pressed into service as a proto-feminist tract.[68] In the tale, the familiar theme of the Transformed Hag, or Loathly Lady, is introduced. Both F. N. Robinson and Helen Cooper agree that the most likely sources for Chaucer were Gower's tale of Florent, the romance *The Wedding of Sir Gawayn and Dame Ragnell*, and the ballad *The Marriage of Sir Gawaine*.[69] In Chaucer's tale, a 'lusty bacheler' in the household of King Arthur, seeing a young woman walking by the riverside, 'rafte hire maydenhed'.[70] Accused before the court of rape, the knight was in danger of execution, but Arthur acceded to his wife's request that the knight's fate should be decided by herself and her ladies. He is given a year to find the answer to the riddle 'What thing is it that women moost desiren.'[71] There follow the knight's adventures, until at the last, he falls in with 'a wyf – a fouler wight ther may no man devyse'.[72] She undertakes to answer the riddle, if he will agree to plight his troth with her. The knight agrees, and they return to the court, where he answers the riddle:

> Wommen desiren to have sovereynetee
> As wel over hir housbond as hir love,
> And for to been in maistrie hym above.[73]

His answer is correct, and he is granted his life. However, the 'loathly lady' steps forward, tells of her part in the solution of the riddle, and demands her reward. The knight must marry her, and consummate the union. Ultimately the knight submits, agrees in future to be governed and led by her, and, on kissing his wife, she is transformed into a young and beautiful woman. The tale ends, as Helen Cooper has it, in marital 'and especially sexual', bliss.[74] 'Bliss' is the operative word, but the ending, it has to be said, is ambivalent, On the one hand the husband is found exultant beneath the bedclothes:

> For joye he hente hire in his armes two
> His herte bathed in a bath of blisse.
> A thousand tyme a-reve he gan hire kisse,
> And she obeyed hym in every thing
> That myghte doon hym pleasance or likying.[75]

But the secret – unexpressed – thoughts and prayers of his wife are rather different:

> Jhesu Crist us sende
> Housbondes meeke, yong, and fresh abedde,
> And grace t'overbyde hem that we wedde;
> And eek I praye Jhesu shorte hir lyves
> That wol not be governed by his wyves.[76]

The Masque of Gwendolen is, as might be expected, less explicit. Gwendolen, 'loveliest of mortal mould',[77] is lusted after by Merlin, who in promises reminiscent of those made by the devil to Christ in the wilderness, offers her reign as 'queen and goddess' in hell, if she will

15

consent to marry him. She refuses, and prays to be made 'a thing of loathing and of natural horror' rather than be the object of his desire. Enraged, he grants her wish, from which she will only be released when 'a youth of form divine, / Sprung from Brutus' ancient line, / Of beauty careless, and delight, / Shall woo thee to the nuptial rite, / Shall his arms around thee twine, / Shall his warm lips press to thine, / And sign thee with the holy sign.'[78]

The next surviving fragment of the masque discloses the now 'loathly lady' Gwendolen asleep in a wooded dell. She is attended by fairies and their queen. Again the inspiration here is the Wife of Bath's Tale, which begins with such a reference:

> In th'olde dayes of the Kyng Arthour,
> ...
> Al was this land fulfild of fayerye
> The elf-queene, with her joly compaignye
> Daunced ful ofte in many a grene mede.[79]

The elf-queen is not named, but in *Gwendolen* she appears as Titania. Here is an infusion from Shakespeare's *Midsummer Night's Dream*, and, just as in Shakespeare's play the fairies sing their queen to sleep,[80] so in the masque they sing a lullaby over Gwendolen. It is interesting to note that the metre chosen by Heber for this verse is that of 'Ar hyd y nos', the Welsh air which he used for his vesper hymn.

Titania is the bearer of good news; Merlin is dead. 'She of the Lake, his elfin paramour, / Jealous of his late wanderings' had imprisoned him within a rock, wherein he had starved to death.[81] Gwendolen, on awakening, is led by a dream to return to Arthur's court, and the scene shifts to Harlech, a castle which, not being too far from Llangedwyn, would have been known to Heber. Here we discover her brother, Llewellin, in chains. He is a hostage for Sir Gawain, who is absent searching for the answer to the riddle –posed in the Wife of Bath's Tale– and posed here by Arthur, that is, what do women mostly crave? If Gawain does not return on this day, then Llewellin dies. Gawain returns, like Mason's Arviragus, in the nick of time, with the solution: What do women mostly crave?

> Power is their passion. From the lordly dame
> To the brown maid that tends the harvest-field,
> They prize it most.[82]

What Gawain does not disclose is that the answer to the riddle, known only to Merlin, he had obtained through Gwendolen, who in her beauty had charmed the secret from the one who had lusted after her. There is, an echo here, perhaps subconscious, of Delilah's cajoling out of Samson the secret of his strength, an Old Testament story which would have been very familiar to Heber.[83] Gwndolen had, in other word, used her 'power' over a man. She had used it again to elicit from Gawain a promise, sworn on his sword, and pledged through the gift of a ring 'to reward my pain / With whatsoe'er I ask'd.'[84] Her refusal to submit to Merlin's desires had brought his curse upon her; now, as Arthur and the court rejoice in Gawain's seeming success, Gwendolen appears as the 'loathly lady', a spectre at the feasts, and demands her reward. Gawain must redeem his pledge. He is forced by his honour to accede to her demand – marriage. (Here Heber is closely following the Wife of Bath's Tale.) Thus the first part of Merlin's curse is lifted; Gwendolen has, however reluctantly, been wooed 'to the nuptial rite' by a youth 'of form divine, / Sprung from Brutus' ancient line', for Gawain is Arthur's nephew. Yet until the marriage is consummated, Gwendolen embraced and kissed by her husband, she is not released from her hag-like form. To her dismay, she finds Gawain determined not to consummate the marriage; he is prepared to grant her rule in his house, governance of his possessions, but not himself. He will leave 'And ramble forth to-night, an errant warrior, / To see thy face no more.'[85] Tearfully, she pleads with him, and he weakens. He promises friendship, he promises that he will not leave, and, finally, agrees 'Come, one kiss of peace / To seal our bargain.'[86] So the second part of Merlin's curse is lifted, again, if Gwendolen's tears may be so interpreted, by the exercise of feminine 'power'. As he kisses her, so she enfolds him in her embrace (the third part of the curse falls), and, in struggling to free himself from the arms of one he believes to be a fiend, makes the sign of the cross. The curse is lifted –to the sound of loud thunder – and the final fragment of the masque ends with the now once-again beautiful Gwendolen calling on Gawain to turn and look upon her. As with the ending of Mason's *Caractacus*, we are left to speculate; for Gawain and Gwendolen, as for Elidurus and Evelina, will they 'live happily ever after?' will love blossom? Shall the marriage be consummated?

Mason's heroine Evelina does not inhabit the same world as Heber's Gwendolen. The former is the epitome of honour, of lofty ideals, pure and in her own way pious, who at no point asks anything for herself.

Gwendolen, by contrast, it can be argued, is manipulative, using her 'power' the power of sexual allure, to prise a secret from Merlin, gain a pledge from Gawain, and force him to redeem it. It has to be said that Gawain himself is by no means without fault. When Gwendolen as the 'loathly lady' presents herself at Harlech, he prevaricates, and threatens to renege on his promise: 'I acknowledge all, / And nobody will repay thee.'[87] He also agrees to marriage, but determines on no more than the form; Gwendolen may be his bride, but will never be his wife, and to ensure that this is the case, announces his intention to 'ramble forth tonight . . . / To see thy face no more.' In modern slang parlance, Gawain intends to 'do a runner'.

Reginald Heber was happily married; his had been a love-match with Amelia, and it remained so. His 'Lines addressed to Mrs Heber', a poem written when he was bishop of Calcutta, is a most moving and beautiful expression of their marital love.[88] Is this the reason why he laid aside his masque, unfinished, in 1816? What he found in the 'Wife of Bath's Tale' was not, as he pondered it, what he understood by, and experienced in, love. The trajectory of his narrative, as it was unfolding, was leading where he did not wish to go, nor which he wished his readers to follow. It was an essentially moral tale, that was in danger of going astray. So he laid down his pen. William Mason, too, made a love-match, in his case in middle age, though it was one tragically cut short by the premature death of his wife. In Mary Sherman he had found the reality of love; although when he wrote *Caractacus* he was still a bachelor don, nonetheless he caught, and expressed in the character of Evelina, the ideal of that love.

Evelina and Gwendolen have now both been almost entirely forgotten, but they deserve better than that, for, whatever their strengths and weaknesses, good points and bad, Mason and Heber brought them to life, they illustrate the place that women were not only taking in the literature of the eighteenth and early nineteenth 'Celtic Revival', but, perhaps also serve as reminders of the place that women were increasingly taking as published authors and avid readers in the same period. Roger Lonsdale, in his introduction to his anthology *Eighteenth Century Women Poets*, noted what he called 'increasing male sympathy for women writers. . .' by the middle years of the century, and reviewers were 'increasingly aware of the importance of women as authors and readers', despite continuing prejudice in some quarters.[89] Certainly women as well as men would have read Mason's *Caractacus*, and would have read Heber's *Masque of Gwendolen*, had it ever been finished. No doubt they did, when his widow published the surviving fragments in her biography of her husband. Lonsdale observed 'In the course of the eighteenth century itself 'polite' taste had increasingly come to favour a poetry of self-conscious elevation above the facts of the mundane world . . .'.[90] Both Mason and Heber were eighteenth century men; it is for the reader to decide whether *Caractacus* and *Gwendolen* support or modify that contention.

Notes

[1] Sam Smiles, *The Image of Antiquity. Ancient Britain and the Romantic Imagination* (London and New Haven, 1994) pp. 47-8.

[2] First published as 'Y Bardd-Celtiaeth a Chelfyddyd' in *Cof Cenedl*, VII, 1992, and reprinted in Peter Lord, *Gwenllian. Essays on Visual Culture* (Llandysul, 1994) pp. 103-28.

[3] Ibid., p. 103.

[4] Gray seems to have begun work on the ode in 1755, but had all but laid it aside when his initial enthusiasm faltered. It was a recital at Cambridge by the blind Welsh harpist John Parry which provided the inspiration for its completion.

[5] Edward D. Snyder, *The Celtic Revival in English Literature 1760-1800* (Cambridge MA, 1923) p. 53.

[6] Paget Toynbee and Edward Whibley (eds), *Correspondence of Thomas Gray* (Oxford, 3 vols, repr. 1971), 2, p. 467.

[7] Snyder, op. cit., pp. 54-5 and p. 54, n.1.

[8] It is the text of a copy of the 1811 edition, held in the Roderic Bowen Library of University of Wales Trinity Saint David, Lampeter, which is used throughout this paper.

[9] Mason's biographer, John Draper, said that *Caractacus* was one of the two plays he wrote which were 'of some moment in the literary and stage history of their day'. The other, as noted above, was *Elfrida*. John W. Draper, *William Mason. A Study in Eighteenth Century Culture* (New York, 1924) p. 172.

[10] Smiles, op. cit., p. 153.

[11] Ibid., p. 153.

[12] Quoted in ibid., p. 151.

[13] Mason acknowledges *The Prophetess* as one of his sources (*Works*, II, note to p. 91, verse 8 on p. 199). It is very unlikely that he did not know *Bonduca*, a play in which Caractacus appears as Caratach. As John Draper pointed out, the plays attributed to Beaumont and Fletcher 'were a vital part of the stage history' of the day. Draper, op. cit., p. 175.

[14] Ibid., p. 176. This is a quite extraordinary assertion, considering that Draper had on the previous page said that Mason 'probably knew' *Bonduca*, and that Mason himself acknowledges his debt to *The Prophetess*.

[15] John Fletcher, *Bonduca. A Tragedy*, in A. R. Waller (ed.), *The Works of Francis Beaumont and John Fletcher. In Ten Volumes* (Cambridge, 1908), VI, pp. 79-159, at p. 112.

[16] Or Andrasta.

[17] Waller, op. cit., p. 112.

[18] Mason, *Works*, II, pp. 97, 98.

[19] Waller, op. cit., p. 123.

[20] Mason, op. cit., pp. 94, 95. It is Mason's biographer, John Draper, who applies the epithet 'ravishing' to Evelina, as used in the title of this paper. Draper, op. cit., p. 183.
[21] The subject of Hayman's 1751 painting.
[22] Toynbee and Whibley, op. cit., II, Letter 216, pp. 464–5.
[23] Smiles, op. cit., p. 80.
[24] The notion of the druids as 'Christian by anticipation' is an interesting one. It is, arguably, easy to see how they could be transformed into the precursors and even 'founding fathers' of what is known as 'the Ancient British Church'. The concept of an 'Ancient British Church' is to be found, for example, in Bishop Richard Davies' introductory letter to the 1567 translation of the New Testament into Welsh. T. Walters (trans.), *The Introductory Letters to the Welsh New Testament first printed in 1567* (Bangor, n.d.) It is also there in one of the Welsh 'Triads' referred to by E. J. Newell in his *A Popular History of the Ancient British Church* (London, 1895) pp. 11–12, in which Christianity is brought 'to the nation of the Cymry' by Bran the Blessed. Bran was, in this tradition, the father of Caractacus, and Caractacus had a sister, Branwen, 'a maiden "divinely fair", whose beauty, gentleness, and woes form the theme of the sweetest and most pathetic of Celtic romances.' (p. 12) The resemblance between Branwen and Mason's Evelina is perhaps, not coincidental.
[25] Stuart Piggott, *The Druids* (London, 1985) pp. 133–4. The whole of chapter IV, 'The Romantic Image' is an important background for understanding the setting of Mason's verse-drama.
[26] There is an interesting, but perhaps unconscious, similarity in the description of the druids' altar in the sacred grove and that built to Jahweh by the prophet Elijah, in his contest with the prophets of Baal (1 Kings 18: 30–2). It is, of course, worth remembering that Mason was himself an ordained priest of the Church of England, who would have been very familiar with this passage. Similarly, when the Romans set foot on Mona, and the sacred island thus 'polluted', the altar is wreathed in smoke, as is the peak of Mount Sinai, at the present of the Lord (Exodus 19: 9). There is little doubt that Mason was depicting Caractacus, the Britons, and the druids as God's chosen instruments to resist the power of the 'pagan' Romans, just as in the mid-eighteenth century he would have seen his own Church of England as the bulwark of liberty and pure faith in the face of the superstition and thraldom of the Church of Rome. It is also worth recalling that Mason was writing when the Jacobite Rising, the '45, the attempt to return the Catholic House of Stuart to the thrones of the United Kingdom, was still fresh in the memory.
[27] Mason, *Caractacus*, pp. 81, 82, 83.
[28] Oliver Davies (ed.), *Celtic Spirituality* (New York, 1999) p. 6.
[29] Ibid, pp. 90–7.
[30] Ibid., p. 98.
[31] Ibid., p. 107.
[32] Ibid., p. 115.
[33] Ibid., pp. 95–6.
[34] Ibid., p. 96.
[35] Ibid.
[36] J. Taylor Hamilton and Kenneth G. Hamilton, *History of the Moravian Church* (Bethlehem, Pa., 1983) p. 155.
[37] Ibid., note to p. 91 verse 8, on p. 199.
[38] Waller, op. cit., *The Prophetess*, vol. 5, 1907, pp. 320–89. Act I Scene III, on p. 328.
[39] Ibid., p. 327.
[40] Quoted by Smiles, op. cit., p. 110.

41 Mason, op. cit., p. 157.
42 Ibid., p. 104.
43 Ibid., p. 88.
44 Ibid, pp. 87, 89.
45 Ibid., p. 116.
46 Ibid., pp. 121-9.
47 Ibid., p. 129.
48 Ibid., p. 131.
49 Ibid., p. 141.
50 Ibid., p. 140.
51 Ibid., p. 146.
52 Elidurus' 'adoption' by Caractacus as his son frees Evelina from the decree of the druids that had been pronounced on Elidurus, and, because of her offer, would have passed on to her.
53 Ibid., pp. 163-74.
54 It was produced at The Royal Opera House, Covent Garden, with incidental music thought to be by Thomas Arne (1710-78), though there is some dispute about this. There is more than a touch of 'patriotism' here (in the sense of a somewhat ostentatious love of country and loyalty to it and defence of its institutions), as there had been about the original verse-drama; it is perhaps worth recalling that Arne had provided the music for James Thomson's 'Rule, Britannia!' of 1740, with its refrain: 'Britons never shall be slaves'. Mason's friend Horace Walpole was not impressed by the performance; he felt it 'no more resembling the manners of Britons than of Japanese.'
55 Sonnet IV, To Bishop Hurd. Mason, *Works*, I, p. 124. Richard Hurd had been consecrated as Bishop of Lichfield the previous year. He and Mason were close friends, and regular correspondents. That friendship is evidenced by his *A Letter to Mr Mason: On the Marks of Imitation* (1757), which includes 'reflections on the pleasures of his years of friendship with Mason, years associated with the "innocent" amusements afforded by poetry.' Not surprisingly, Hurd was also friendly with Thomas Gray. Sarah Brewer (ed), *The Early Letters of Bishop Richard Hurd 1739-1762* (Woodbridge, Church of England Record Society, 1995) p. xv.
56 Draper, op. cit., p. 176 (and n.27) and p. 128.
57 Once again, there is an element of 'patriotism' here. The opera, which was well received, was first performed during England's wars with Revolutionary France, at that date an avowedly atheistic state.
58 Da Ponte, a far from satisfactory priest, in the latter part of his life settled in the United States, where he became Professor of Italian Literature at Columbia College (later University). He is credited with the libretti of 28 operas by eleven different composers. Rodney Bolt, *Lorenzo Da Ponte. The Extraordinary Adventures of the Man behind Mozart* (London, 2006) pp. 251, 252. Bolt does not mention the opera's 'pre-history' in Mason's verse-drama.
59 Snyder, op. cit., pp. 193-4.
60 Ibid., p. 196.
61 ODNB sub. nom. The poem was subsequently set to music by William Crotch.
62 The Calcutta bishopric then encompassed the whole of India, and stretched as far as Australia as well. Heber died of a cardiac arrest in his bath. He was only 43.
63 Reginald Heber, *Miscellaneous Poems*, pp. 253, 254, 261.
64 'Marwolaeth yr Esgob Heber', printed in O. M. Edwards (ed.), *Gwaith Alun* (1909), pp. 101-6. I am grateful to my friend Wyn Thomas for this reference.

65. Blackwell was a native of Mold, Flintshire, and later rector of Manordeifi. His elegy for Heber won the prize at the 1828 Denbigh eisteddfod. *The Welsh Dictionary of Biography*, p. 39.
66. Amelia Heber, *The Life of Reginald Heber, DD* (London, 2 vols, 1830), vol. 1, pp. 449-59. In the *Miscellaneous Poems* the masque appears on pp. 192-207. It is this latter printing and pagination that is followed here.
67. Amelia Heber, *Life*, 1, pp. 448.
68. For example, Marion Wynne-Davies, *Women and Arthurian Literature. Seizing the Sword* (London, Macmillan Press, 1996), discusses the tale from a feminist perspective.
69. F. N. Robinson, *The Works of Geoffrey Chaucer* (Oxford, 1957) p. 703. Helen Cooper, *The Canterbury Tales* (Oxford, 1989) p. 157.
70. Line 888.
71. Line 905.
72. Lines 998-9.
73. Lines 1038-40.
74. Cooper, op. cit., p. 156.
75. Lines 1252-6.
76. Lines 1258-62.
77. *Miscellaneous Poems* (hereafter *MP*) p. 193.
78. *MP* p. 197.
79. Lines 857, 859-61.
80. Act II, Scene II, lines 9-32.
81. *MP* p. 199.
82. *MP* p. 204.
83. Judges 15: 4-20. Heber would also have known John Milton's *Samson Agonistes*.
84. *MP* p. 205.
85. Ibid.
86. *MP* p. 206.
87. *MP* pp. 204-5.
88. *MP* pp. 289-90.
89. Roger Lonsdale (ed.), *Eighteenth-Century Women Poets* (Oxford, 1990) pp. xxxi, xxxii.
90. Ibid., p. xliii.

'CHRISTIAN SINCERITY': THE REVEREND HENRY HANDLEY NORRIS AND PAROCHIAL MINISTRY

Figure 2: Henry Handley Norris.
Portrait by Thomas Phillips, RA. Reproduced by courtesy of the
Rector of St John of Jerusalem Church, South Hackney.

The work and influence of what subsequently came to be known as 'The Hackney Phalanx' in the Established Church of England in the early years of the nineteenth century has been well documented.[1] In this context, the central and oftentimes seminal role of Henry Handley Norris, its unofficial leader, in the work of the Society for the Promotion of Christian Knowledge (SPCK), the National Society for the Education of the Poor in the Principles of the Established Church, and the Incorporated Church Building Society, has long been recognised. The 'Phalanx', as Mark Smith pointed out, was never a Society in and of itself or an organised 'party', but in reality a group of like-minded friends in some cases related by marriage,[2] with common theological and pastoral concerns. Here Norris's gift for friendship was crucial. His almost lifelong attachment to Joshua Watson (1771–1855) and to Watson's brother John James, with whom he shared long years of ministry in Hackney, is well known, but the circle of friends included Edward Churton, Archdeacon of Cleveland; Herbert Marsh, successively Bishop of Llandaff and of Peterborough; William Van Mildert, Marsh's successor at Llandaff and subsequently Bishop of Durham; and Christopher Wordsworth, Master of Trinity College, Cambridge. There were others less closely attached, for the 'Phalanx' was never an exclusive club, and these included two archbishops of Canterbury, Charles Manners Sutton and William Howley; Thomas Sikes, Rector of Guilsborough; and Edward Churton's father Ralph, who was appointed Archdeacon of St Davids by Bishop Thomas Burgess, who, seen in this light, may himself have been on the fringes of the Phalanx. These were all scholarly men, who, as Mark Smith asserts, 'placed a high value on the integrity of the visible church [as] the primary channel of saving grace first transmitted through baptism and nourished by the sacrament of the Eucharist and good works, and on holiness of life.'[3] It is this latter concern, holiness of life, seen as an essential ingredient of effective pastoral ministry, which this paper seeks to explore in respect of Henry Handley Norris, as heretofore it has received less attention than his more 'public' activities. But first it is necessary to say something of his early years and formation.

I

Norris was a Londoner; his father, also Henry Handley Norris, was a city merchant engaged in trade with Russia, who was married to Grace, the daughter of the Revd Thomas Hest, Vicar of Warton in Lancashire from 1775–89. Henry, born on 14 January 1771 in the parish of St Andrew Undershaft in the heart of the City, was their only son, and therefore heir to his father's considerable fortune and estate.[4] As such, it might have been assumed that Norris would follow in his father's footsteps, but, as a letter dated 9 November, 1789, from his tutor Thomas Ingle to Henry, senior, would indicate, at the age of eighteen, the young man was undecided as to his future, though his inclination lay elsewhere than in trade. Ingle said:

> My view in [sic] a Coll: Education is to furnish him with the means of providing an income for himself to live upon, and not to depend wholly on me for support!!! (This remark raises the possibility that Ingle was in some way related to the Norris family, otherwise it is somewhat puzzling.) If he is intended *for the Church*, [his emphasis]

a better plan could not in all probability have been adopted, nay, a University Education is a necessary step, especially necessary since the Bishops in the south insist so particularly upon it. They will not ordain a young man that has not graduated at one of the universities.

Ingle went on:

He seems as you once told me, to have a wish to go into the Church, and says, he knows you will buy him a living, but I'm confident he has not made up his mind and his choice is still to be made.[5]

Thomas Ingle since 1788 had been a Fellow of Peterhouse, Cambridge, but was resident in Edinburgh in 1789, as the address on this letter confirms, where he had been studying medicine for a three-year period under Dr Charles Brown and Dr William Cullen, two of the leading physicians of the time, and in a university renowned for its medical faculty.[6] Ingle was to graduate MD, and at Peterhouse become the Tutor in 'Physic'. His reference to Norris having 'not made up his mind' does perhaps raise the possibility that at this date the young man was himself thinking of following a career in medicine – as a physician, which required a university education, rather than as a surgeon, which did not, though there is no supporting evidence for this suggestion. There is some evidence, albeit indirect, that Norris's father was opposed to his entry into the ordained ministry. Thomas Mozley, who was personally acquainted with Norris, wrote that one very closely related to him – by which it can be assumed it was his father – was so opposed, which caused the young man distress, but that he was supported in his intent by his grandfather.[7] It has to be said that Ingle's letter to Norris's father, saying that Henry, junior 'knows' that his father will buy him a living rather gives the lie to Mozley's assertion. Given that the young Henry was the heir to his father's established business and estate, there can be some sympathy for his father's reluctance to support him, if indeed he was, and on the surviving evidence this seems unlikely.

As far as the ordained ministry in the Established Church was concerned Church patronage, an advowson, was property and as such could be bought and sold as well as inherited. Certainly Henry Norris, senior, was sufficiently wealthy to have purchased 'the next turn' of the patronage of a suitable living for his son once canonically ordained, as Ingle indicated. In the event H. H. Norris senior did not follow this path.

Ingle's other point, about the necessity of a University education as a prerequisite is, in the light of research by Sara Slinn, of some interest.[8] Slinn's analysis of the educational status of ordinands to the diaconate in the 1790s bears out Ingle's observation. The highest percentage of graduates is to be found in the dioceses in the southern Province of Canterbury; the lowest in that of York.[9] So a university education, an assured income, and suitable character, would effectively guarantee Henry, junior's, acceptance for ordination, in all probability in his home diocese of London.[10] And the last 'qualification' he seems to have possessed:

> As to Henry himself . . . he does not appear to me likely to launch out into dashing, his first appearance in Hall was rather the reverse; he is extremely neat in his appearance but very far from what we call a Blood . . .[11]

Norris had initially been admitted as a pensioner at Pembroke College, Cambridge in 1788, but by the time Ingles was writing to his father, had migrated to Peterhouse. He graduated BA in 1793, and MA in 1796, by which date he had indeed 'gone into the Church', being ordained deacon in that year. It was however before then, in Hackney, no doubt on a visit from Guilsborough where he was preparing for ordination, in June 1794, it is said that he met the son of another wealthy London merchant, Joshua Watson, when both became involved in organising a subscription for a company of Shropshire militia then stationed in Hackney.[12] It is easy to forget that 1794 was something of a crisis year for Great Britain and for the government of William Pitt. The country had been at war with Revolutionary France since February, 1793; the military situation in 1794 has been described as 'daunting', with the possibility of invasion in the forefront of the minds of many, and there were rumblings of discontent if not outright rebellion at home and in Ireland.[13] With regular troops deployed elsewhere, much of 'home defence' lay with the militias, hence the deployment of that from inland Shropshire to an area close to the vulnerable Thames waterway.[14] These were men a long way from their homes and families, and men like Norris and Watson were quickly responsive to their needs. According to Peter Nockles the 'inseparable lifelong' friendship and alliance between the two – Norris and Watson were both 23 – dates from this time.[15] However it is unlikely that 1794 marked their first acquaintance as both the Norris and Watson families were residents of Hackney and would have attended the same parish church. The two young men were alike in being serious-minded and devout Christians. They were appalled and dismayed by what was happening in France, where Christianity to all intents and purposes had been 'abolished' by the Revolutionary government in June 1793. The friends were apprehensive of the spread of such an ideology at home and Nockles maintains that Norris in particular 'developed a deep-rooted horror of Jacobinism or "French principles" from an early date.'[16]

Norris, as noted earlier, was ordained deacon in 1796,[17] on a title to Stretton-on-Dunsmore, as assistant curate to the Revd John Sawbridge, who also became a lifelong friend. Norris had first made his acquaintance during the time between his graduation and ordination whilst staying with and studying under one of Sawbridge's friends, Thomas Sikes, the vicar of Guilsborough.[18] (Norris was to retain an affection for Stretton; in 1812 he presented a window to the church.)[19] Three years later, in 1799, Joshua Watson's brother John James became the incumbent of Hackney, and Norris moved back to his home parish to assist him. Hackney was to be the focus of his pastoral ministry for the rest of his life.

II

Norris's first publication, as was to be the case of many of those which followed, was of a sermon, which he had preached on 22 November 1801, in St John's Parish Church, Hackney. Entitled *The Influence of the Female Character upon Society*,[20] it is rather dismissed by Peter Nockles as containing 'much colourful invective against the immodesty of the "poisoned garments" then being imported and copied from the "Grecian" female fashions of late revolutionary France, which was indeed the case.'[21] Nockles sees this as evidence of Norris's marked antipathy towards the 'subversive forces unleashed by the French Revolution', which, he believed, would undermine the social, political and religious morality and stability of England. This judgement is reinforced by Norris's choice of text, 1 Peter 3: 1–3, but the thrust of Norris's exposition, based on an analysis of a catena of biblical texts, is on what he calls 'the influence of the female character' in society, and how high a calling and responsibility that is. Of signal importance here, he maintained, was the true vocation of the female to promote 'holiness and virtue' in society. The New Testament gospels, Norris emphasised, also provide ample evidence of the loving loyalty of women to Christ:

When the disciples forsook our Saviour and fled, did not the women continue with him, careless to provide for their own safety, when their Lord was in danger? (Matt. 26: 56 and 27: 55 compared) Were not they the last to take leave of him when he was dead, and the first to welcome his resurrection? (Luke 23: 55 and 24: 1 compared).

He reinforces his message by saying

> the care of the female members of the infant church would not have been looked upon as a matter of such moment, as both the history and epistles represent it, had they not contributed very greatly, by their active piety, to the advancement of the Christian faith. Nor would St Peter, in my text, have attributed to their conversation the surprising power of winning even those whom the word could not convert, had he not himself been witness to many instances, wherein it had so mightily prevailed.

Further, modifying Nockles's assertion, Norris is not so much concerned with the condemnation of contemporary female fashion, though that is there, as to emphasise:

> The church, the spouse of Christ, is described by the psalmist as having her clothing of wrought gold, so are the virgins that be her fellows, and bear her company, represented in raiment of needlework, [She should be] all-glorious within. This is her characteristic excellence; and she requires it of those that attend upon her, that whilst they neglect not external attractions, their chief attention be devoted to the adorning of the hidden man of the heart, in that which is not corruptible.

Again and again Norris returns to the responsibility of the female members of the church to set an example, a persuasive example as he sees it, of piety, loyalty to Christ, and courage.

III

This 1801 sermon, preached when Norris was thirty years of age and had been in Orders for only five years shows evidence of a maturity of style, knowledge of scripture, and an ability to marshal his evidence in the advancement of his argument. This was something that was to be characteristic of most of his publications thereafter. The long appendix to the published version of the 1801 sermon reveals something of Norris's choice of, and approach to, his subject. It is clear – and he freely acknowledges this – that the theme of his address was inspired by the 4th edition of 'Professor Robison's *Proofs of a Conspiracy*' combined with 'Mr Windham's *Address to the Throne Approving of the Preliminaries of Peace with the Republic of France*',[22] which he had read and digested. The *Proofs of a Conspiracy* was the work of John Robison (1739–1805), a versatile scientist and inventor, whose varied academic career had included a period as Professor of Mathematics at Kronstadt, in the empire of Catherine the Great, and the chair of Natural Philosophy at Edinburgh University.[23] His most popular publication proved to be his *Proofs of a Conspiracy against all the Religions and Governments of Europe carried on in the Secret Meetings of Freemasons, Illuminati, and Reading Societies*, first published in 1796, and which had reached its fourth edition, that cited by Norris, in 1798. Although received with scepticism and a degree of embarrassment by some of his fellow scholars, it was welcomed by others, and has been seen as a founding text of conspiracy theory.[24] Norris certainly seems to have found the argument convincing as Robison's assertions would have re-enforced the deep suspicions of atheistic Revolutionary France which he and his close friend Joshua Watson held, and which were referred to earlier. The subject thus suggested, chosen and embarked upon, in its exploration of these 'primary sources' Norris added references to the Classical world (Hesiod and Simonides, Menander and Euripedes), the early church (Clement of Alexandria), more recent literature (Addison, Dryden, St Evremont), and what might be termed 'secondary sources' – Bishop Potter's *Grecian Antiquities*,[25] Sale's *Koran*,[26] and Prideaux's *Life of Mahomet*,[27] all obviously drawn from his wider reading. The overall result was a well-crafted and argued essay-sermon, which would have been appreciated by an educated middle-class audience, even if some of the passages had made rather uncomfortable hearing or reading. Similar judgements can be made in respect of his subsequent published sermons and addresses.

His emphases on piety, on holiness of life and virtue is not just empty rhetoric, evacuated of meaning – such can all too easily become no more than trite expressions. That this was not the case can be demonstrated by two other works; one, an unpublished sermon dating from 1799, and the other, his *Memorial for the Parish Priest*, first published anonymously in 1815. The former,[28] *The Majesty and Advantages of Prayer*, one of his few unpublished sermons to survive, shows very clearly what Norris understood by piety:

> The man who does not *pray*: does not live; he may walk about, and seem to be alive; but he does not live in the plain sense of the Word; for as the natural breath is a proof that the body is alive; so the breath of prayer is a proof that Religion is alive in the heart.

That prayer includes, but is not confined to, the public worship offered by the church. Whilst admitting that 'the custom of praying with the church at all the regular times of prayer [is] *one* of the methods of prayer *always* [his italics], "praying always" was essential in the life of the Christian: also 'With those that pray, God is present; and if God be not present with a man we know who will be . . .' he warns.

In his *Memorial for the Parish Priest*, intended as its title makes obvious, for his clerical brethren, he nonetheless includes material which is useful for the laity. For example, it is here that he refers to private prayer as a 'duty'.[29] He also recommends retreat, time for quiet reflection and self-examination, and reading. The Christian, and especially the Christian minister, should not be taken up with unnecessary 'busyness'. 'There is a habit I strongly recommend to my younger brethren to attain early in life; that is, the habit of solitude; to be able, comfortably, to pass a series of days without society.'[30] 'Always have a book at hand to fill up the straggling minutes.'[31] Such reflections as these fill out our understanding of Norris's definitions of the Christian life, and 'piety'. At no time, then or subsequently, did he fall victim to that cloying sentimentalism which was to characterise (enervate and undermine} so much of mid- and late nineteenth century 'pietism'.

IV

In 1804, with the death of his father, Norris became financially secure and independent. His circumstances were to remain, at the very least, comfortable for the rest of his life. One of the first-fruits of his inheritance was the erection of a proprietary chapel in south Hackney, towards the cost of which he made a substantial contribution, and which he served *gratis*. Dedicated to St John of Jerusalem – somewhat confusingly, as Hackney Parish Church was also dedicated to St John – it became a perpetual curacy in 1806, in which year he further endowed it. A watercolour of 1830, by M. A. Gliddon, shows this church to have been a severely plain 'box', relieved only by a portico over the principal entrance, surmounted by a 'pepper box' turret. To this he added at his own expense a house for the minister in Well Street.[32] As indicated earlier, this is not the house in which Norris himself resided. When the Revd Thomas Mozley dined with him in 1834 he described the family estate as illustrated by Toussaint:

> a large and comfortable house – parsonage or not I do not remember. It seemed quite in the country, standing in the midst of thirty-five acres of green fields, plantations, and full-grown hedge-rows. One could hardly see a roof or a chimney to remind one of the metropolis. There was something like a farm-yard, with a large haystack, near the house. We walked out and looked around. Norris was thankful he had been the means of reserving all this open space from the invasion of builders. He said nothing of its future.'[33]

Norris obviously lived in some comfort; Mozley makes mention of his carriage, and also of a butler, who presided over the meal.'[34]

There is no doubt that, financially and socially secure as he was, Norris nonetheless thought deeply about his responsibilities as priest and pastor. One aspect of that ministry to which he gave serious attention was preaching. Effective preaching, he believed, required careful and prayerful preparation. In his *Manual for the Parish Priest*, he devoted some space to this. For example, he looks at both style and content. In respect of the former, he counsels 'Guard against that uninterrupted flow, which archbishop Hort observes "glides like a smooth stream over the soul, leaving no traces behind it."'[35] In addition, he says, 'the language of a sermon cannot be too *plain*, but it may be too *familiar*' [his emphases].[36] Such advice is ageless, and any reading of Norris's own sermons shows that he adhered to his own principles. Fluency of expression can easily conceal paucity of content, and 'plain-speaking' is not the same thing as chattiness.[37] Nor do his sermons 'parade' the research and reading that lie behind them; the preparatory work of the library and the study remains there, and is not referred to from the pulpit.[38] Only in the appendices to the published versions of the sermons, in themselves substantial essays, does Norris reveal and discuss his sources.

This structure is again apparent in his sermon published as 'A Scriptural Investigation of the Doctrine of the Holy Places' preached on 28 December, 1828 and 4 January 1829 in 'the Church and Chapel of St John at Hackney' in aid of the Society for the Repairing, Enlarging and Building Churches.[39] The sermon as published runs to 34 pages to which Norris added a Preface of eight and Appendices of 21. It is here, in Appendix II, that Norris expounds the fascinating theory that the *locus* of the Last Supper was an upper room in the house of Nicodemus, and that it was here that the disciples continued to meet, where the Risen Christ appeared to them, and where the earliest celebrations of the Eucharist, in obedience to the Dominical Command, took place.[40] In the sermon itself Norris reveals his ability to hold the attention of his hearers through the use of a striking observation. Speaking of the Jerusalem Temple, he reminded his audience that it was intended that, as Isaiah had proclaimed, it should be 'the house of prayer for all people,'[41] and that within its walls was a court 'specially prepared for the Gentiles'. It was this provision that was being profaned by being made 'a den of thieves'[42] by the activities of the money-changers, and it was this profanation, Jesus by his action, cleansed and overturned. Nonetheless the Temple in its totality, the Lord prophesied, was 'doomed to desolation', and He proclaimed that 'where two or three were gathered together in His name, there was He in the midst of them – *there* was the Temple, not in its material substance . . . but "in spirit and in truth."'[43]

V

For Norris effective and informative preaching was important, but it was only part of the pastoral responsibility of the priest. In his *Manual for the Parish Priest* he quoted with approval Bishop Gilbert Burnet's injunction 'He understands but little of the nature and obligations of the priestly office who thinks he has discharged it by performing the public appointments.'[44] Norris had no time for such formalism. In addition to the *Manual* much can be learned of his understanding of the pastoral responsibilities of the priest from the sermon that he preached in Hackney Parish Church on 23 June 1839, being the Sunday following the funeral of his great friend and co-worker, John James Watson, and his own reflections on his nearly forty years of ministry which are contained in an unpublished sermon delivered to his own congregation.[45] The former, on the text of John 10: 11, and entitled 'The Good Shepherd' is a distillation of his own thinking, and it is to be suspected that of Watson, the result not only of conversations between them, but also of Watson's own Charge in his capacity of Archdeacon of St Albans to the clergy of his archdeaconry in 1826, but which remained unpublished until the year of his death.[46]

Entitled 'The Divine Commission and Perpetuity of the Christian Priesthood' Watson's Charge was a robust and forthright defence of the Church Catholic and, as he understood and believed it to be, the place of the Established Church of England within it. The church's fundamental doctrines and teachings, received from apostolic, sub-apostolic and conciliar times, were immutable and inviolable: 'The Church being the Church of God, it can never be in the power of man to remodel it after his own devices' he asserted; the church could not be subject to fashion or the tool of innovation.[47] Such was anathema; 'They who have never been undeceived in the prevailing delusion that the Church may be *any thing*, [his italics] are soon led, by a very easy transition, to conclude that it may be *nothing*.'[48] In modern parlance, 'those who stand for nothing will fall for anything'. He bewailed the fact that 'there is no one article in our Creed less frequently enforced, and, of necessary consequence, less understood and less attended to, than that in which we profess our belief of the Holy Catholic Church.'[49] It is worth noting that Watson's warnings to his clergy pre-dated by more than six years John Keble's famous Assize Sermon, which is generally accepted as firing the 'starting gun' of the Oxford Movement and Archdeacon Watson's words were to be echoed by his friend and collaborator, Norris, in his 1835 sermon 'Neutrality in time of Danger to the Church, an Abandonment of the Faith, and very Short-Sighted Worldly Policy. An Admonition to the Members of the Church of England' preached in his church at South Hackney.[50] It is this assertion, or, perhaps re-assertion, of the church's doctrine, order and place in society which underpins Norris's explorations of the meaning, purpose and emphases of what might be termed 'ministerial priesthood' and the pastoral responsibilities of the clergy.

In his 1839 reflections on the ministry of his friend Archdeacon Watson, Norris expounds his understanding of the meaning of the designation 'the Good Shepherd'. 'As the office of herdsman or shepherd was . . . important, so we find it was considered one of trust and continuance, not committed to hirelings.'[51] So the 'cure of souls', delegated by a bishop to the priest of a parish involved mutual trust, trust between the Chief Pastor, the bishop, and his priest, and trust between the priest and the community committed to his charge. It was also one of 'continuance'; time was necessary for that mutual trust to take root, grow and flourish. Norris viewed with at least disfavour clergy who spent but a short time in one place before moving on – a practice, to be fair, that was not characteristic of the nineteenth century church. He warned that the good shepherd should not necessarily expect an easy life: 'As it was a service of trust, it was not infrequently a service of danger.'[52] The dangers that might confront the parish priest were not likely to be those that had confronted Jacob in his twenty-year care of Laban's flock,[53] but nonetheless he should expect and have the faith to confront hostility and hardship in the discharge of his responsibilities. Down through the centuries, the role of the good shepherd remained the same:

> As in the time of the fathers He designed to communicate this title [Good Shepherd] to the men whom He appointed 'shepherds of His flock', so still in the Church He has left those to whom His pastoral charge is given, whose office it is to lead His people into green pastures, and assuage their thirst by the waters of comfort.[54]

It was also necessary for the good shepherd to understand the nature and composition of his flock. 'The sheep of Christ are a "flock", not a number of disconnected individuals' Norris reminded his hearers.[55] 'Together with the sheep, the Lord enjoins the care of the lambs of the flock, as a charge of equal consideration, and His tender solicitude for children, that they should be brought to Him, was manifested by many moving incidents in His life.'[56] Norris's lifelong concern for education, and his intimate involvement in the work of the SPCK in particular, are both well known, and need no further emphasis here. What is important in this context is his understanding that the role of the parish priest as good shepherd involved care and concern for all of those who made up his flock, sheep of all ages, and lambs together, and this involved on-going concern and nurture: 'It is not in the mere providing of folds for the lambs of Christ that the good shepherd's concern for them is terminated' – the provision of church buildings and schools was not an end in itself – 'superintendence afterwards is still more essential to their welfare.'[57]

In July 1848, in his sermon preached after nearly forty years of ministry in South Hackney, Norris returned to this theme, this time preaching on the text of 2 Corinthians 11: 2, which he had used, as he says, 'when on first entering upon my spiritual charge among you,' *For I am jealous over you with godly jealousy; for I have espoused you to one husband, that I may present you as a chaste virgin to Christ.*[58] This text, Norris told his congregation, 'tells every minister of souls, who is put in trust with the charge of a portion of Christ's household, that his office is that of the Paranymph or companion of the heavenly Bridegroom, to bring with him the souls of those whom by his labour in the word and sacraments he has "espoused to Christ".'[59] He then goes on to consider in more detail the role and responsibility of Christ's companion:

> To [the] love of God our Saviour towards men it is our blessed office, as His ministers, to be subsidiary; – it is the title in which His saintly forerunner rejoiced, – to be "the friend of the heavenly Bridegroom", we may not claim dominion over your faith, but we covet to be helpers of your joy; to be your servants for Jesus' sake, to introduce you to that state which shall be perfected in His far exceeding and eternal might and glory.[60]

The role of the friend of the heavenly Bridegroom was, in essence, to be 'servus servorum Dei', exercising thereby the persuasive ministry outlined in the Ordinal of the Book of Common Prayer that it was the responsibility of priests to be 'messengers, watchmen, and stewards of the Lord; to teach and to premonish, to feed and provide for the Lord's family . . .' and that [the priest] should 'never cease your labour, your care and diligence, until you have done all that lieth in you, according to your bounden duty . . .'[61] Of particular importance, Norris felt, was the responsibility of the pastor to warn his flock against what he called 'those errors of opinion, of which the world judges so lightly.' These 'do indeed in many cases dishonour God in the highest attributes, and bring unhappy men to deny the Lord that bought them.' So, he warned his people, 'Make not yourselves judges of the word of God, nor seek to bend it to men's opinions, for that word shall judge you in the last day.'[62] Of the 'word of God', Holy Scripture, Norris had the highest opinion: in one of his occasional and memorable phrases, he referred to the biblical writers as 'the penmen of the word of God.'[63]

As noted earlier in this paper, underpinning every aspect of the pastoral ministry, as Norris understood it, and expounded it in his preaching and writing, was the necessity of prayer, private as well as public. It was an understanding that remained with him throughout the ensuing years.

VI

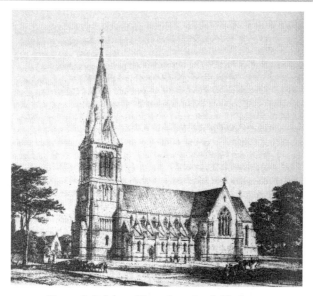

Figure 3: St John of Jerusalem, South Hackney.
Lithograph by the architect, E. C. Hakewill, 1845. Reproduced by
permission of the Rector of St John of Jerusalem, South Hackney.

Did Norris himself exemplify what he so consistently emphasised? Edward Churton, Archdeacon of Cleveland, in his sermon preached in St John's, South Hackney, on 15 December 1850, the Sunday following Norris's funeral, and entitled 'Christian Sincerity' certainly thought so.[64] Churton (1800–74) was the son-in-law of John James Watson, whose daughter Caroline he married, and he had been Watson's curate at Hackney from 1830–4. Through his marriage Churton had become friendly with his wife's uncle, Joshua Watson whose biography he was to write and also with Norris and other members of the 'Hackney Phalanx'. The son of Ralph Churton (1754–1831), appointed Archdeacon of St Davids in 1805 by Bishop Thomas Burgess – although he had no Welsh, no prior connection with that diocese, nor ever resided within its borders – it was from his father that Edward inherited his uncompromising churchmanship.[65] In respect of Norris, Edward Churton could, therefore, speak with some authority of someone he had known for twenty years as friend and mentor, and whose theological and ecclesiological outlook he shared.

Churton's sermon of 1850 is dedicated to Charles James Blomfield, Bishop of London, who is described by the preacher as having shared with Norris a 'long-tried friendship . . . maintained . . . for a long and uninterrupted series of years.'[66] The printed version of the sermon covers 28 pages, and is followed by an Appendix of five, detailing the moves to provide a permanent memorial to Norris in his church. Churton took as his text Psalm 15: 1, *Lord, who shall dwell in thy tabernacle? Or who shall rest upon thy holy hill?* He urged his hearers to 'think of those whose souls are now at rest, those who have spoken to you the word of God, and warned you of the deceits and disappointments of the unquiet world, who both in their life and death "have set-to their seal that God is true".'[67] The measure by which the Christian is to be judged is Christ Himself:

> In His most holy life we must study the full meaning of the character of a righteous servant of God; and with that life we must compare each particular both of what is approved and what is forbidden. And in proportion as they approach that pattern, must we account of those who have humbly followed His blessed steps in the path of truth and uprightness.[68]

Such is the life of 'Christian Sincerity' – 'sincerity towards God and man, – a hearty love of Truth for its own sake – the revealed Truth of God first and then truth between man and man . . .'[69] Churton went on to share with his hearers his understanding of the nature of Truth:

> A holy distain of all deceit and vileness, – a ready honour for all, in whatever rank of life, who are swayed by a righteous fear of God – an unswerving integrity in the midst of a corrupt and evil world, – a zeal for righteousness, shining forth more strongly when the righteous cause may seem to be oppressed – and words of faithful counsel, whether of warning or encouragement, to all that are known to stand in need of them. Such sincerity and faithfulness with a constancy and fortitude which secures them in the midst of dangers to the unstable and irresolute, appear to be the qualities which pervade each particular of duty described in this animating psalm.[70]

All of these characteristics, Churton asserted, were exemplified by Norris; he was a man 'converted to the Truth',[71] his Christian sincerity 'removed from careless indifference or light inconstancy',[72] as one who stood against what he deemed the 'widespread disaffection for the central truths of Christianity.'[73] There had been a time, only recently past, if indeed past it was, when:

> The Gospel itself had been too often preached as little more than a more perfect code of morals, and the study of its heavenly mysteries had been discouraged as only tending to provoke dispute, or nourish fanaticism. Or, when these things were not forgotten, there was yet a disposition ... to preach 'Christian godliness without Christian order', and to exalt preaching above prayer and sacraments. It was a state of things which had gone near to divide what Christ had joined together, and it is no wonder if religious men in those days began to question, whether the Church was able to make converts from the evil that was in the world.[74]

Norris, said Churton, in his daily ministry swam determinately against that tide. He was, 'zealous for the faith',[75] not wasting 'his solitary hours in the pursuit of curious trifles, the busy idleness of men without an aim in what they read: but as Nazianzen says of Basil "his life was the guide of his studies; and his studies the seal and attestation of his life."'[76] (Churton, through his reading of the Fathers of the early Church, was well aware not only of the deep and enduring bond of friendship which endured between St Gregory Nazianzen and St Basil, the kind of friendship which was a cement of Christian fellowship, but felt that it was also something which was aspired to and exemplified by members of the Hackney Phalanx.) It was this focus of his thought, prayer and study which gave a notable clarity to Norris's explaining and expounding the Gospel, something to which the extracts from his sermons, published and unpublished, and his other writings, bear witness. As a pastor he was approachable, affable, lively, and courteous, 'innocently gay, when the bow was unstrung – but always with an inclination to speak, when the company would allow, of something which concerned religion and the Church, of piety or charity.'[77] Such an inclination, Churton said, was there 'because the care of them was deeply seated in his heart'.[78]

There can be little doubt that Norris possessed the respect and affection of many of his parishioners, as well as of his wide circle of friends. He had used his personal fortune to provide and endow schools within his parish, and founded and funded the church of St John of Jerusalem, South Hackney, and served it *gratis* as its priest, as well as contributing munificently to its replacement. Churton reminded his hearers of Norris's ability to gain the trust of young people, and the pains that he took in preparing candidates for Confirmation. In a long passage in his *Manual for the Parish Priest*,[79] Norris made a distinction between the formal process of catechesis and preparation for Confirmation; the latter was particularly concerned with what might be termed 'Christian formation'. For Norris his parishioners were 'a pastoral company ... sustained by [Christ's] perpetual presence with them',[80] and the nurture of the faith of the young was an important part of the responsibility with which the pastor of that 'company' was charged. The priest had to know his people; Norris in his *Manual* emphasised the importance of regular pastoral visiting, not just of the sick. 'By entering into all their little cares and troubles, and, as far as he is able, relieving their distresses with his advice and assistance,' through 'constant communication', the parish priest is enabled to become acquainted with the different characters of his people and encourage them to come to him 'in all their wants and perplexities.'[81] Only by such means could the priest gain the trust of his people, and provide the necessary occasions for strengthening them in the faith. He was an advocate of self-examination, and, when necessary, of auricular confession,[82] and felt strongly that 'the duty of private prayer may be more powerfully urged in a domestic visit than in a sermon'.[83] In self-examination, it was necessary to be mindful that 'if we measure ourselves by ourselves, we shall not be wise';[84] the Christian's measure is Christ. Above all, it is necessary that the Christian be reminded that 'Christianity is not morose or ascetic, that the Gospel considers man as a social being, not abstracted and solitary; that it teaches us to *use the world* and not *abuse* it [his emphases]; to resist and overcome temptation, not flee from the trials which the Almighty sees fit to prove us in this life, to prepare us for the life to come.'[85]

It is this constant reference to the Person of Christ, and to the gospels that explains Norris's opposition to the work of the Bible Society. As Peter Nockles rightly pointed out, that opposition was grounded in his firm conviction, expressed in a 4 March 1813 letter to Ralph Churton, Archdeacon of St Davids, that Holy Scripture was not, 'in the purpose of God the instrument of conversion – but the repository of divine knowledge for the perfecting of those already converted. I mean that it is the children's bread and not to be cast to dogs.'[86] The language is forceful as well as biblical but it embodies an important and very often overlooked essential truth. Norris was here re-iterating what is expressed in the 1662 Book of Common Prayer Collect for the Second Sunday in Advent:

> Blessed Lord, who has caused all holy Scriptures to be written for *our* learning: Grant that *we* may in such wise hear them, read, mark, learn, and inwardly digest them, that by patience and comfort of thy holy Word, *we* may embrace and ever hold fast the blessed hope of everlasting life, which thou hast given us in our Saviour Jesus Christ. [my emphases]

These words would have been as familiar to Ralph Churton as they were to Norris. The Collects were – and are – the 'putting into public and corporate form the petitions of the people' gathered together with their priest for the purpose of corporate worship; an expression of the prayer of the Christian faithful in that context. So Norris was correct in his assertion, which was entirely in accord with the expressions in the Advent II Collect.[87]

VII

Although friendly with the long-serving Prime Minister, the Earl of Liverpool, who sought his advice on appointments to the episcopal bench, Norris steadfastly refused to accept a bishopric himself.[88] His only preferment, other than South Hackney, was to a prebendal stall at Llandaff Cathedral (St Dubritius, 22 November 1816) and another at St Paul's Cathedral (Holbourn, 4 November 1825), both of which he held until his death, although on the foundation of the Additional Curates Society in 1837 he made over to it the proceeds accruing from them.[89] His Llandaff prebend – a diocese and cathedral with which he had no previous connection – he accepted with some reluctance from his close friend Herbert Marsh, who had been consecrated its bishop only three months previously. Marsh had inherited a diocese that had drifted into somnolence during the protracted episcopate of his predecessor, Richard Watson, and also a cathedral chapter that was dominated by Watson's friends and relations, many, like himself, mainly resident in the Lake District.[90] The vacation of the prebend of St Dubritius by the pluralist Dr Benjamin Hall provided Marsh with the opportunity of making what proved, because of his own early translation to Peterborough, to be his only appointment to the Chapter, probably not just as a gift to his friend (the St Dubritius prebend was not an especially well-endowed one) but also in the hope that Norris would be able to inject some new life into that body.[91] Norris was on very good terms with Marsh, and also with his successor at Llandaff, his friend from within the Hackney Phalanx William Van Mildert, but not with Edward Copleston, who followed Van Mildert after his translation to Durham. Writing to a friend, the Revd the Hon. A. P. Perceval in 1841, Norris took his Diocesan to task:

> Two sermons recently published by the Bishop of Llandaff in which he lays it down "never to have been" declared by any of its four Churches confessions or formularies that Episcopal Ordination is *essential* [his emphasis] or indisputable, and follows this up by an aversement that we regard it (the ordination of Priests who have been themselves duly ordained) as an approximation to the perfect rule and venture not to declare that it is 'ineffectual' nor presume to say that there can be no real Sacraments – no Absolution – in short, no Church where the Episcopal Order is wanting, altho' we know it to have been the original constitution.[92]

Although the text of this letter is somewhat confused, his indignation and argument are clear enough – and clear enough to distance him from the Bishop of Llandaff. The feeling was clearly mutual; in only one of his letters does Copleston mention Norris, and it is not complimentary. Writing to the Revd Bruce Knight on 15 September 1831, Copleston said 'How shameful a practice it is to give these little things [i.e. the prebendal stalls at Llandaff] to people no way connected with the Diocese. Fleming, Gaisford, Norris, James – what earthly pretence have they to eat up these morsels away from the hungry & ill-fed clergy of the Diocese.'[93] Although his diocese was to benefit financially from the work of the Additional Curates Society, Norris's making over of the income of his Llandaff prebend to that body probably did not mollify the bishop. In contrast, Norris's relations with his London Diocesan, his long-term friend Charles Blomfield, were close and harmonious.

Henry Handley Norris may be seen as exemplifying the best of the pre-Tractarian 'High Churchmanship' within the Church of England. He was never entirely at home with Tractarianism, and increasingly suspicious of what he saw as a 'Romeward' trend in some of its leaders.

He distanced himself, for example, from Pusey's Eucharistic theology, being closer in spirit to that of Daniel Waterland, whose works had been edited by his friend William Van Mildert.[94] As time went on he became an increasingly marginalised figure; something he realised, and which is perhaps exemplified by the increasingly tetchy and querulous nature of his correspondence. Death came to him peacefully and relatively speedily. In the autumn of 1850 he suffered a paralytic stroke, from which he never recovered, dying before the year was out.[95] In many ways he was a man of his time, and in others he had probably outlived his own. J. F. C. Harrison reminded his readers that 'socially the gulf between a vicar with an income of as much as £1000 a year and a handloom weaver with 12/- a week if he were lucky, was felt to be too great to allow of any common interests.'[96] There is an element of truth in this, but it is too sweeping a generalisation. Norris was a wealthy man, and he certainly, as Mozley pointed out, made sure that the increasing urbanisation of South Hackney did not impinge too closely on his own home, where he lived, as we have seen, in some comfort. But the bulk of his fortune was devoted to the care and nurture of the people committed to his charge, who he strove to serve to the best of his ability. It cannot be argued convincingly that he was any less welcome in the homes of his poorer parishioners than he was in those of the better off. He never sought advancement in the church into which he had been ordained, and refused it or accepted it with reluctance – as in the case of his Llandaff prebend – when it was pressed upon him. He remained mindful of what he himself had written at the very beginning of his *Manual for the Parish Priest*: 'If the priest be inattentive to his duty; the religion of the people will grow cool or corrupt; their moral conduct will become depraved, and the civil, as well as the ecclesiastical, polity will be [in] danger.'[97]

Notes

[1] See for example, Peter B. Nockles, *The Oxford Movement in Context. Anglican High Churchmanship 1760–1857* (Cambridge, 1994); Kenneth Hylson-Smith, *High Churchmanship in the Church of England from the Sixteenth Century to the late Twentieth Century* (Edinburgh, 1993), especially pp. 101–20; and Mark Smith, 'Hackney Phalanx' in the *Oxford Dictionary of National Biography* (hereafter cited as ODNB).

[2] For example, H. H. Norris's great friend and fellow-worker in Hackney, the Revd John James Watson (1767–1839) married Caroline, the sister of the wine-merchant, Baden Powell (1767–1841) who was a Hackney resident. Baden Powell's daughter, Henrietta, married Norris. Another daughter of Baden Powell, Susanna, married the Revd Thomas Sikes, the

Vicar of Guilsborough, with whom Norris stayed whilst preparing for ordination, who was thus his brother-in-law. J. J. Watson's brother, and Norris's lifelong friend Joshua, married Sikes's sister Mary. Baden Powell's son and namesake, the Revd Baden Powell (1796–1860), Norris's brother-in-law, was a pioneer physicist who, although an early supporter of the standpoint of the members of the Hackney Phalanx, became an increasingly radical theologian. (Pietro Corsi, ODNB – sub. nom.)

3   ODNB 'Hackney Phalanx'.
4   He was also something of an antiquary, publishing 'On the Cubical Contents of the Roman Congius' in the 1782 *Archaeologia*. Bodleian Library, Oxford, MS Eng.C.7202. Norris Papers. The congius was the Roman equivalent of the gallon. The Norris family home was, and had been for several generations, in south Hackney. A sketch of *c*.1840 by G. Toussaint shows a substantial three-storey eighteenth century mansion, set in mature grounds. The sketch, made in H. H. Norris's lifetime, is of the house he continued to occupy throughout his South Hackney ministry. Geoff Taylor, *A Parish in Perspective. A History of the church and parish of St John of Jerusalem, South Hackney* (London, 2002) p. 13, reproduces the sketch. I am grateful to the present rector, the Revd Andrew Wilson, for providing me with a copy of this work.
5   Bodleian Library, Oxford, MS Eng.C.7202. Norris Papers.
6   Brown recommended Ingle to Cullen as one who possessed 'a great character from his college, where he is much esteemed as a gentleman and a scholar.' Unfortunately, Brown confided, he had 'the misfortune of being very deaf' and hoped that Cullen would be able to help him. Cullen was then 79, and died the following year.
7   Thomas Mozley, *Reminiscences, Chiefly of Towns, Villages and Schools* (London, 2 vols, 1855) 1, p. 54.
8   Sara Slinn, *The Education of the Anglican Clergy 1780–1839* (Woodbridge, 2017).
9   Ibid., p. 59. Only the poor diocese of St Davids, then in the province of Canterbury, where a mere 7.3% of ordinands were graduates, does not fit the overall picture.
10 Here 77.7% of ordinands to the diaconate in the 1790s were graduates, and a further 8.9% described as 'students'. Slinn, op. cit., p. 59.
11 Ingles to Norris, op. cit. This reference to dining in Hall at Peterhouse would seem to indicate that Ingles, whilst pursuing his medical studies in Edinburgh, did, in fact, spend some time resident in Cambridge as well, otherwise it is difficult to understand what is obviously based on 'first hand' observation.
12 Watson's father, John (d. 1821) was a wine merchant, with his counting-house in Tower Hill. Joshua joined his father in business in 1786 and became a partner in 1792.
13 See, for example, the account given by William Hague, *William Pitt the Younger* (London, 2004), especially chapters 17 and 18.
14 The Shropshire Militia was one of the volunteer regiments deployed in southern England to reinforce local defences in areas deemed to be either possible invasion sites, or threatened areas.
15 ODNB sub. nom.
16 Ibid.
17 The Norris Papers contain a letter, dated 31 October, 1796, from Joshua Watson at an address in Mincing Lane, London, congratulating his friend 'upon the accomplishment of your wishes'. Bodleian Library, Oxford, MS.Eng.C.7202.
18 Mozley, op. cit., 1, p. 56. Stretton is to the south-west of Rugby, Guilsborough to the east. The two parishes are a good twenty miles distant one from the other. Bodleian Library, Oxford, MS.Eng.C.7202 contains a set of verses, dated 12 September 1801, and addressed

to 'M. M. Sikes of Guilsborough', which, taken with 'A Non-descript between an Ode and an Epistle' of 24 November 1795, in the same collection, shows that Norris, however competent he was in prose composition, was no poet; both effusions are the most appalling doggerel.
19 Thomas Mozley, *Reminiscences, Chiefly of Towns, Villages and Schools* (London, 2 vols, 2nd edn, 1885), 1, p. 141.
20 Printed for F. & C. Rivington, London. The sermon itself comprises 35 pages, to which is added an Appendix of 24.
21 ODNB sub. nom.
22 This was the Rt Hon William Windham (1750–1810), MP for Norwich.
23 For an outline of the career and significance of Robison, see Paul Wood's assessment in the ODNB.
24 I am grateful to Professor William Gibson for providing me with a copy of this work. It is perhaps worth noting in relation to some of the conclusions of the *Proofs of a Conspiracy* that Robison was in poor health for nearly the last fifteen years of his life, and for part of that period at least increasingly dependent on laudanum to relieve his pain, though his thorough research into, for example, European Freemasonry, remains of value.
25 John Potter (c.1674–1747), successively Bishop of Oxford and Archbishop of Canterbury. His *Archaeologia Graecae* appeared in two volumes, 1697 and 1699, and was frequently reprinted. See L. W. Barnard, *John Potter, An Eighteenth Century Archbishop* (Ilfracombe, 1989).
26 George Sale (1697?–1736) Arabic scholar and supporter of the SPCK. His pioneering translation of the Koran first appeared in 1734.
27 Humphrey Prideaux (1648–1724), Dean of Norwich. His literary reputation rests largely on this work, first published in 1697.
28 Bodleian Library, Oxford, MSS Eng.E.3455–6.
29 *Memorial for the Parish Priest, being a Few Hints on the Pastoral Care, to the Younger Clergy of the Church of England, from an Elder Brother* (London, 2nd edn 1822) p. 127. Describing himself as 'an Elder Brother' is somewhat tongue-in-cheek; Norris was 44 when this work first appeared!
30 Ibid., p. 20.
31 Ibid.
32 In 1825 the Church Building Commissioners established three rectories in Hackney – Hackney, South Hackney, and West Hackney. However, somewhat puzzlingly, on the title page of a sermon published in 1829 Norris is described as 'Perpetual Curate of St John's Chapel'. Not until 1835 does he appear as 'Rector of South Hackney.'
33 Thomas Mozley, *Reminiscences. Chiefly of Oriel College and the Oxford Movement* (London, 2 vols, 1862), 1, p. 338.
34 Ibid., pp. 338, 339. It seems that by this date Norris tended to fall asleep at the dinner table once the ladies present had withdrawn, to the consternation of his guests. It was the responsibility of the butler to gently reawaken him once tea was ready to be served in the drawing-room!
35 *Manual for the Parish Priest*, p. 71. The reference is to Josiah Hort (1674?–1751), Archbishop of Tuam, author of a number of works of instruction for his clergy, sermons and charges.
36 Ibid., p. 72.
37 The published sermons of, for example, Laurence Sterne, *The Sermons of Mr Yorick* (The Works of Laurence Sterne, Cambridge, for The Jenson Society, 1906) often exemplify the former failing. However, in fairness to Sterne, his published sermons, not by any means all delivered to parochial congregations, are too uneven in quality to justify too sweeping a

judgement. It is next to impossible to judge the impact of a sermon as and when preached if all that is available is a written or printed text.
38 This lies behind his injunction 'Nothing gives such clear and correct ideas upon a subject as putting down the thoughts on paper.' *Manual for the Parish Priest*, pp. 62–3.
39 The inference from the title page is that the sermon was preached in both the Parish Church of St John, Hackney, and Norris's own Chapel of St John of Jerusalem, South Hackney. It was published by Rivingtons in 1829.
40 1829 sermon, Appendix II, pp. 41–56.
41 Isaiah 56: 7. Repeated by Jesus, as recorded in all three of the synoptic gospels.
42 The phrase was first used by Jeremiah (7: 11) in the context of the profanation of the Temple.
43 1829 sermon, pp. 19–20.
44 *Manual*, p. 84.
45 Oxford, Bodleian Library MS Eng. E.3456. The text is 2 Corinthians 11: 2.
46 J. J. Watson, *Charge to the Clergy of the Archdeaconry of St Albans at his Primary Visitation, 1826* (London, 1839). The see of St Albans was not founded until 1867; in Watson's time his archdeaconry was within the diocese of London.
47 Watson, *Charge*, p. 17.
48 Ibid., p. 12.
49 Ibid., p. 11.
50 Printed by J. G. & F. Rivington in 1835.
51 *The Good Shepherd. Sermon on the Sunday following the Funeral of the Ven. J. J. Watson, Hackney Parish Church, 23rd June 1839* (London, 1839) p. 6.
52 Ibid., p. 7.
53 Genesis 31: 39–40.
54 *Good Shepherd*, p. 11.
55 Ibid., p. 13.
56 Ibid., p. 22.
57 Ibid., p. 23.
58 Oxford, Bodleian Library MS Eng. E. 3456. By this date work was effectively complete on the building of the present St John of Jerusalem Church in South Hackney, designed on a large scale by E. C. Hakewill, the foundation stone of which was laid in May, 1845. The new church, on a different site from the old, cost the huge sum of £160,000 to construct. It was consecrated by Bishop Blomfield of London in July, 1848. Norris's sermon was therefore among the first, if not the first, he preached in the new church. Taylor, op. cit., pp. 25–37, with illustrations of the building.
59 Ibid, f. 5.
60 Ibid., f. 12.
61 1662 Book of Common Prayer. The Form and Manner of Ordering of Priests.
62 1848 sermon, f. 17.
63 Ibid., f. 6.
64 Published by Francis and John Rivington, London, 1851.
65 As indicated earlier, Burgess may well have been more sympathetic towards the standpoint of the 'Hackney Phalanx' than is generally realised. Archdeacon Ralph Churton named one of his sons, Henry Burgess Whitaker Churton (b. 1810) after him. Ralph Churton's *A Short Defence of the Church of England* (1795) encapsulated much of the thinking shared by his son Edward.
66 Letter Dedicatory, unpaginated.
67 1850 sermon, p. 10.

68 Ibid., p. 11.
69 Ibid., pp. 11–12.
70 Ibid., p. 12.
71 Ibid., p. 14.
72 Ibid., p. 15.
73 Ibid., p. 16.
74 Ibid., pp. 16–17.
75 Ibid., p. 19.
76 Ibid., p. 18. Churton's reference is to St Basil the Great (d. 379) and his great friend St Gregory of Nazianzus (d. 389).
77 Ibid., pp. 24–5.
78 Ibid., p. 25.
79 *Manual*, pp. 74–83.
80 Sermon 1839, 'The Good Shepherd', pp. 12–13.
81 *Manual*, p. 120.
82 Ibid., p. 23; Churton, op. cit., vol. 2, p. 239.
83 *Manual*, p. 127.
84 Ibid., p. 162.
85 Ibid., pp. 159–60.
86 Nockles, op. cit., p. 200.
87 K. D. Mackenzie, 'Collects, Epistles and Gospels', in W. K. Lowther Clarke and Charles Harris (eds), *Liturgy and Worship* (London, 1964) pp. 374, 382. This particular Collect for Advent II first appeared in the 1549 Book of Common Prayer.
88 During his premiership Liverpool was responsible for more than twenty appointments to the episcopal bench. With the exceptions of William Howley (London 1813), Thomas Burgess (Salisbury 1825), Herbert Marsh (Llandaff 1816 and Peterborough 1819), William Van Mildert (Llandaff 1819 and Durham 1826) and Charles Blomfield (Chester 1824), it is difficult to discern any direct link between Norris and those appointed. Marsh and Van Mildert were prominent members of the Hackney Phalanx, and both Howley and Burgess at least sympathetic. Blomfield was a personal friend. The translation of Burgess, whose sight and mental powers were both failing by 1825, from the widespread diocese of St Davids to the more compact and less demanding see of Salisbury, could be deemed an act of compassion, and may even have been suggested by Norris's friend, and Burgess's archdeacon of St Davids, Ralph Churton. The vacancy thus created was filled by the promotion of Lord Liverpool's own cousin, the scholarly, shy and somewhat reclusive John Banks Jenkinson.
89 Edward Churton, *Memoir of Joshua Watson* (Oxford & London, 2 vols, 1861), vol. 2, p. 53.
90 See my 'Bishop Richard Watson and his Lakeland Friends', *Transactions of the Cumberland & Westmorland Antiquarian & Archaeological Society*, 77, 1977, pp. 139–44.
91 For Marsh's episcopate at Llandaff, see Roger L. Brown, 'Herbert Marsh, Bishop of Llandaff 1816–19' in his *Llandaff Figures and Places* (Welshpool, Gwasg Eglwys y Trallwng, 1998) pp. 1–11. Like Norris, Marsh was a strong supporter of SPCK, and highly critical of the work of the Bible Society.
92 Pusey House, Oxford, Library, Bound volume, *Rev H. H. Norris and Archdcn. Churton to Hon & Rev A. P. Perceval*. Norris's relations with Perceval were to cool somewhat during the 1840s, as he believed Perceval was more inclined towards certain leaders of the Oxford Movement, especially E. B. Pusey, than he was himself.

[93] Roger L. Brown (ed.), *The Letters of Edward Copleston, Bishop of Llandaff, 1828-1849* (South Wales Record Society, 2003), p. 81. Of the canons mentioned by Copleston, only John Fleming (St Andrews 1800-35) was a survivor from Watson's episcopate. Edward James (St Cross 1827-54) and Thomas Gaisford (Fairwater 1823-55) were both appointed to the Chapter by Bishop Van Mildert. James, Norris and Gaisford all retained their canonries throughout Copleston's episcopate, and into that of his successor, Alfred Olllivant. John Fleming is of some interest; wealthy and well-connected, he was Rector of Bootle, Lancashire 1814-35, but resided mainly on his estate at Rayrigg, neighbouring that of Bishop Watson at Calgarth, whose chaplain he was. He also acted as assistant curate to his kinsman, the Revd. Sir Richard le Fleming, Bt., the Rector of Grasmere and Windermere 1823-57. He is buried in Windermere churchyard with members of his family, and close to Bishop Watson. His third son, and namesake, was the incumbent of Ponsonby, Cumberland, and vicar of the Llandaff Chapter living of Llangwm, Monmouthshire, where he died and was buried in 1857.

[94] Van Mildert edited the works of Daniel Waterland, published in ten volumes in 1823. For Waterland (1683-1740) see Robert T. Holtby, *Daniel Waterland 1683-1740. A Study in Eighteenth Century Orthodoxy* (Carlisle, 1966), and for his Eucharistic theology in particular, C. W. Dugmore, *Eucharistic Doctrine in England from Hooker to Waterland* (London, SPCK, 1942), especially pp. 169-83. For Van Mildert himself, see E. A. Varley, *The Last of the Prince Bishops. William Van Mildert and the High Church Movement of the early nineteenth century* (Cambridge, 1992), in which there are numerous references to Norris.

[95] Churton, op. cit., vol. 2, pp. 288-9.

[96] J. F. C. Harrison, *Early Victorian Britain, 1832-51* (London, 1988) pp. 124-5.

[97] *Manual*, p. 1.

'THE COUNTRY IS ON THE MOVE': THE REVDS J. W. WELSH, F. H. W. SCHMITZ AND THE S.P.G. MISSION TO EMIGRANTS FROM LIVERPOOL[1]

I

It is estimated that in the one hundred years between 1830 and 1930 an astounding nine million emigrants sailed from the port of Liverpool, primarily bound for the United States of America, Canada and Australia.[2]

For much of this period Liverpool was, by far, the most important port of departure for emigrants from Europe because, as well as its established transatlantic links, Liverpool was well placed to receive the many emigrants from the countries of north-western Europe, such as Scandinavians,[3] Russians and Poles who crossed the North Sea to Hull by steamer and then travelled to Liverpool by train. Irish emigrants crossed to Liverpool by steamship... By 1851 it had become the leading emigration port in Europe...

Inevitably, this resulted in Liverpool experiencing a constantly changing influx of temporary residents, those awaiting the departure of the ship that was to transport them to their new life in America or the antipodes. Geoffrey Best has drawn attention to what he called the 'moral fibre' of those who uprooted themselves from their familiar and familial surroundings, and prepared to leave these shores; those who 'required positive moral strength and a willingness to do violence to all those traditional affections, loyalties and attachments upon which the mid-Victorian moralist, in any other context, set peculiar binding value.'[4] Having made the decision, and removed themselves to their port of embarkation, the potential emigrant found himself in a bewildering and sometimes hazardous situation. 'Emigrants were not allowed on board their ships until the day before, or the actual day of sailing, so this meant that most emigrants usually spent between one and ten days waiting ...'.[5] Men, women and children, uprooted from familiar surroundings, had little or nothing to do but wander the streets, with the likelihood of falling victim to the enticements to be found in any port city. Liverpool's emigrants had one thing in particular to contend with. They 'were liable to harassment and fraud by local confidence tricksters, known as "runners". Runners frequently snatched the emigrants' luggage and would only return it if the emigrant paid a large fee.'[6] Already impoverished emigrants were thus liable to losing most if not all of their scanty resources. Then there was the question of accommodation; the emigrants had to find shelter whilst awaiting the departure of their ship. Until 1852 the only resource available was a lodging house, and that facility was 'often inhospitable, dirty and overcrowded'.[7] The situation was eased somewhat in 1852 for one group when an emigrant depot and hospital for those departing for Australia under Government auspices was opened in a converted warehouse complex in Birkenhead.

Apart from the physical needs of those departing these shores, there were the spiritual. The local churches and chapels were not in a position to deal with these; the scale of the problem can be illustrated by the statistic recorded in February 1855 that in the previous year some 4,000 people a week were passing through and boarding the ships in the Mersey.[8]

The Society for the Propagation of the Gospel (SPG) was all too aware of the challenge, and in 1849 had appointed the Revd J. W. Welsh as Chaplain to Emigrants from Liverpool. John William Welsh was a nongraduate, who had been educated in Dublin, and prepared for ordained ministry at St Aidan's College, Birkenhead. He was made Deacon in 1849 and ordained Priest in 1850 by the Bishop of Chester, John Graham, in whose diocese Liverpool then lay, to serve the Emigrant Chaplaincy for SPG. Welsh was required, by the terms of his appointment, to submit quarterly reports of his ministry to SPG Headquarters, and those from November 1854 until May 1858 survive in the SPG Archive, now housed at the Bodleian Library in Oxford. Welsh was an assiduous correspondent, and his accounts provide a vivid picture of his ministry, a demanding and almost ceaseless round of activity, which was not without risk. Welsh had a real talent for telling his story, and an ear for accents, especially Scots and Irish. His reports form the first part of the paper which follows.

II

From 1852 Welsh's operational base was the Emigrant Depot at Birkenhead, though he was personally accommodated at St Aidan's, the Church of England Theological College in the town, where he had been prepared for his ministry.[9] The Depot had been formerly Warehouse A1 of the Dock Company. There was 'a large, well-ventilated, dining hall', which could seat 600, and which could be speedily adapted to form a place of worship. The hall was divided into three 'schools', the English, Irish and Scottish emigrants being segregated. Evidently there was some mutual distrust between the groups, perhaps owing to religious and denominational differences. The depot finally closed in 1868, by which time an estimated 180,000 had passed through it, en route to the antipodes.[10] Emigrants for Australia from Birkenhead fell into two categories; those of a 'private character', who were nonetheless under the surveillance of Government officials, and those wishing to emigrate under the protection of the government, and at the expense of the colonies. (The government in Australia had secured funding from the sale of Crown Lands, a portion of which was remitted to the United Kingdom to commissioners based in London, who used the monies to assist those applying for passage.) Applicants for such an assisted passage were means-tested, having to contribute between £1 and £5, and be assessed for age, occupation and character. Rations were allocated for the voyage. The commissioners advertised for tenders for ships to transport the successful applicants, and employed surveyors to examine the ships for seaworthiness and suitability. Some three or four ships a month sailed from Birkenhead under these arrangements, which means that the emigrants spent rather longer at the Depot than those sailing from Liverpool across the Mersey.[11] Welsh's time was thus divided between a somewhat more 'settled' group of aspiring emigrants at Birkenhead, and the much larger 'floating' population of those waiting only a matter of days at most to leave from Liverpool.

In his first surviving report, dated 12 November 1854, Welsh makes mention of 'the awful pestilence which raged so fearfully amongst my people during the summer and autumn.'[12] His reference is to what is sometimes called the 'Third Invasion' of Asiatic cholera in the United Kingdom.[13] Not as severe as the two preceding, the outbreak nonetheless claimed some 30,000 lives, more than 10,000 in London alone.[14] Despite the best endeavours of its Medical Officer of Health,[15] Liverpool, with its overcrowded housing, did not escape, suffering as it had done in earlier outbreaks.[16] In 1832, for example, there had been 5000 recorded cases of cholera, of whom 1500 died, and this in a population of 230,000.[17] The figure did not include those emigrants who succumbed on voyage. As Norman Longmate graphically put it: 'the track of many a vessel across the Atlantic was marked by a trail of bodies wrapped in sailcloth and bundles of infected bedding dumped overboard.'[18]

The cholera outbreak had added to Welsh's work, but clearly the day-to-day ministry to the emigrants had continued unabated. Aided by members of a 'Ladies' Committee', he visited those awaiting their voyage in the Lodging Houses, and visited the ships in the Mersey as they prepared to sail, holding services on board, 'on one occasion preaching to 400–500 passengers on one ship.' In his next report, dated February 1855,[19] he enlarged somewhat on this, saying that 'In fine weather he could assemble all passengers on deck for Divine Service, but in cold and wet had to go below, and repeat the service several times' – something, not surprisingly, which left him exhausted at the end. Below decks, the passengers were divided into three; single women were accommodated aft, single men at the bow, married couples and children in between. This segregation explains why Divine Service had to be repeated.[20] In his February 1855 report Welsh gives a breakdown of the emigrants sailing from the Mersey: '210,742 persons sailed... as emigrants in the past year, that is, more than 4000 a week'. For 'the conveyance of this multitude of people, composed of the surplus population of at least three European nations, a fleet of 957 ships has been employed'. Of those sailing, 194,922 were bound for the United States, 'chiefly Irish and German'; 41,491 were bound for Australia; about 20,000 for the colonies of 'north America' (i.e. Canada); about 200 to the East and West Indies. On May 12 of the same year,[21] he noted that daily departures were of some 400 souls, 'down by about 200 over earlier years', but still an impressive average of approximately 12,000 a month. These, he commented, were of a 'much better class than in former years', and the majority were females, perhaps travelling to join male partners who were already settled, and had sent for them. However, that some may well have been hoping to secure a partner on arrival – one has to remember the 'fishing fleets' to the Indian sub-continent in this respect – cannot be discounted.[22]

Numbers continued to fall during the summer of 1855, down to about 300 a day according to his next report, dated 12 August.[23] However, 'nothing human can put a stop to the movement. There is now hardly a poor family in the kingdom without some relative in Australia or America who is continuously encouraging them to "come out" to him.' Therefore, the ship-visiting went on, not without its hazard to life and limb. In this August report Welsh bewails the risk entailed, not so much from the waters of the Mersey but from the boatmen he had to employ to travel from shore to ship, and ship to ship. There was, he said, 'the difficulty I have in procuring steady, sober boatmen . . . They are a most dangerous class of men. They are still at liberty to make any charge they please when one is anxious to leave a vessel as she is about to sail; and I have frequently been in imminent peril of my life on finding myself in the middle of a dangerous river in a small boat with men too drunk to pull an oar or set a sail.' Still, there were compensations; in November he noted that on leaving one vessel, the emigrants lined the rails and called 'Three cheers for the Queen, and three for the Church of England'. Gratified, Welsh admitted, this 'made my hair almost stand on end'.[24]

The decline in numbers during 1854 and 1855 it would seem was largely due to the Crimean War. With the cessation of hostilities, and the subsequent peace, emigrant numbers began to climb again, to nearly 1000 a week.[25] In May 1856 Welsh reported 'hundreds are again walking up and down, endeavouring to find the first and biggest vessel for New York or Melbourne'.[26] By August, Welsh had reached his '29th Quarterly Report'.[27] Numbers of emigrants continued to rise; '3,000 left Liverpool in July, 1856'. In this report he focused on the plight of the sons and daughters of Irish gentlemen 'who have lost their estates'. He instanced one young man, aged twenty, who was accompanied by his sisters and elderly mother. 'The young ladies were intending to enter into service, while their brother hoped to procure a situation as a coach or omnibus driver, as he could do nothing else.' As the young man himself put it, 'And I hope to be happier by labouring for my bread than my unfortunate ancestors have been in Ireland for ages – borrowing money and living years in advance of their incomes.' Presumably, the combination of the depredations of the famine, a hopelessly financially encumbered situation (his family would not have been alone in their class in Ireland in being close to bankruptcy), the activities of the Irish Tenant League, and the death of his father, had led the young man to give up the fight, and seek a new, and less fraught if humbler, life for himself and his dependants in the United States, Canada, or Australia.

In the late 1850s, Welsh reported on the continuing rise in the number of emigrants passing through Liverpool, 127,558 in the months before

August, 1857.[28] New Zealand was now figuring as a destination; in 1855 no ships had cleared the port for that destination, but in 1856-7 some 1,136 emigrants, all English, had sailed, aiming to settle there.[29] His 'deck services' as he described them, short and to the point (the Litany, or a Psalm, followed by a sermon), continued, but sometimes had their problems. In August 1857 he had needed an interpreter, as his congregation had consisted largely of monoglot Gaelic-speaking Highlanders. There was also some opposition to his ministry. In his earliest surviving report, that of November, 1854,[30] he had mentioned what he described as 'a confrontation' with three ecclesiastics from Maynooth, the Catholic seminary in Ireland, and a minority of Irish Catholics continued to cause occasional problems. In February, 1858, for example, he mentioned a group which had disrupted one of his on-board services by 'loudly reciting the Rosary'.[31] This 'aggressive piety' as he called it, was not permitted on 'Government Ships', but was evidently tolerated or ignored on commercial sailings.[32] He seems to have had more trouble with Irish Catholics waiting at the Birkenhead Depot than with those already on board. In November 1855 he reported that prospective emigrants at Birkenhead, from Tipperary and Clare, 'seemed wholly given up, as a mass, to dancing, fighting, thieving and card-playing, drink being out of their power in the depot'. Yet every cloud had a silver lining; there was 'always a small body of quiet Christian people amongst them, members of the Church of Ireland, to whom it was perfectly delightful to minister.'[33] Welsh, whose Dublin education almost certainly identifies him as an Anglo-Irishman and an adherent of the Church of Ireland, was, at this date, given his upbringing, at the least rather uncomprehending of the Catholic Irish. Certainly, his rather censorious judgement upon them was far from being an isolated instance, witness the somewhat similar and almost contemporaneous verdict passed by Welsh emigrants as recorded by Professor Bill Jones.[34] Many of the Welsh migrants, from a strict Calvinistic Methodist background, were scandalised by what Huw Walters called the 'wild Irish and surly Germans'[35]. Then there were the Mormons; by 1857 they were providing funds to aid emigration to Utah. One prospective emigrant, he reported, had four wives with him, two of whom were sisters. The Mormons he encountered were chiefly from Manchester, Rochdale and London, and active in proselytising.[36] Then there was the problem of ignorance; so many of the emigrants had had little or no contact with organised religion, and no knowledge of Christian teaching. 'One could not tell me the difference between a sacrament and an Apostle', he lamented, and another 'believed our Saviour was an Englishman who was very good to the poor'.[37]

In 1862 Welsh's long and arduous ministry in Liverpool and Birkenhead was coming to an end, though he did not relinquish it until 1864, and he reflected upon what had been achieved, and what qualities his successor would need to have to continue the work.[38] He recorded that his efforts had, in the main, been supported by the goodwill of the Emigrant Officers, the ship-owners, and the ships' captains. He gave more detail of his deck services; he was received on board, the ship's bell was tolled for Divine Service, and the passengers assembled on deck. The capstan was covered with the Union Jack, or some other national flag. This he used as his Reading Desk and pulpit, and the congregation sat on spars, casks, or the bulwarks – holding on to the rigging. Of his congregations, he said they were 'homeless ones, strangers to me and to each other, with real earnestness in their looks, and an unmistakeable fervour in their united responses.' He had often administered Baptism, and celebrated the Holy Communion on shipboard, this last below decks, and using a small table covered with a linen cloth. There were often as many as one hundred communicants at a time. There were also sad times; disease, including typhus, took its toll, and he had ministered at many death-beds, both in the lodging-houses and on board ship, having thereafter to officiate at the funerals. He also gave more details of his ministry at the Birkenhead Depot, where he held a daily service at 7.30 p.m., the emigrants sitting on forms from the Dining Hall or on their own "emigrants' boxes" for the prayers, and his sermon or lecture. This brought his day, often an extremely demanding and exhausting one, to an end, especially if it was one where he had had the problems with the boatmen, as described above. Here, he adds, almost *en passant*, that he had 'more than once had to swim for my life'.

Regarding his potential successor, Welsh was of the opinion that he should not be too young, should have some experience in ministry to agricultural classes (who made up a large percentage of those emigrating) having 'made himself acquainted with their habit of thought'. It was essential that the candidate be able to speak and preach at a moment's notice: 'It is absolutely a *sine quae none* that he be an extempore preacher.' He suggested a stipend of £250 per annum, and concluded, 'The post of chaplain to emigrants will continually prove to be the binding principle by which our poor brethren who go out to the colonies are kept united to the church of their fathers. Indeed, I consider it one of the most important of the Society's Missionary Stations.' He could not resist adding 'It is a sphere, however, in which a man must be content to work unnoticed by the church.' [his underlining]. Certainly his own fifteen years as the Emigrant Chaplain at Birkenhead and Liverpool did not result in ecclesiastical preferment; in 1864 he was licensed as assistant curate in the parish of St Nicholas, Liverpool, and as chaplain to the Anfield Cemetery, work which kept him in touch with the Emigrant Service, for in the latter capacity he was primarily involved in the burial of paupers and homeless potential emigrants, and ministry to the bereaved families. He was still engaged in that ministry a decade later.

II

After 1854 the Revd J. W. Welsh did not have to work alone, for at the beginning of that year his ministry was complemented by that of the Revd F. H. W. Schmitz. Schmitz was an equally interesting, and perhaps rather more colourful, character than Welsh. A somewhat unusual combination, he was a German in Anglican Orders, and after ordination in 1839, had served as an SPG Missionary in India, at Madras (1839) and Tanjor (1844). He was thus somewhat older, and more experienced, cleric than his *confrere*. Married, he eventually became an emigrant himself, for after 1858 he was in the United States of America, as the founding pastor of a German Lutheran congregation, St Peter's at Delphos, meeting in a small school building belonging to the Methodist Church. The outbreak of the Civil War saw him enrolled as a military chaplain, in the German regiment from Cincinnati, the *Die Neuner,* in which a former regular officer in Prussia, August Willich, held a senior command. In August, 1861 Willich was instrumental in forming the 32nd Indiana Volunteers, for the Union against the Confederacy, of which he was the elected colonel, and it is primarily with the 32nd that Schmitz was associated, seeing active service, for example on the battlefield at Missionary Ridge.[39] The last record of him so far traced dates from November, 1863, when he was still a military chaplain. Thereafter he passes out of history.

Schmitz was employed from early 1854 as 'chaplain and Government Interpreter to Germans at Liverpool', a role for which he was particularly qualified. If his reports, or 'Journal' as he described it, are anything to go by, his written English, at least, was clear and fluent. His energy is apparent in the early entries of the journal for 1854. Apart from the 'bread and butter' ministry, of visiting the lodging houses and distributing tracts and books, on 13th February he records the securing, with the help of Mr Welsh, of a large hall for Divine Service, though he notes that some months would need to elapse before he could use it, as he did not have the means to fit it up.[40] He had also secured for himself the honorary office of Interpreter to the Government Emigration Authorities, which, he said, would 'give him greater influence and enable him to visit ships in the river free' – something that Welsh, as we have seen, found was otherwise expensive. (Schmitz calculated it could cost as much as 3-5/- to board a ship in the river; a substantial sum.) Like Welsh, he had fallen foul of the 'Runners', 'of which', he said, 'there is a goodly number in Liverpool'. These gangs were 'disappointed and displeased' at the support his work was receiving from the merchant community, and also from Captain Schomberg, RN, the Government Emigration Officer. 'No doubt', he observed, the Runners 'will annoy me occasionally, as I am an obstacle in their way to their continuing to cheat the poor Emigrants which has been hitherto carried on here to a fearful extent'.[41] His ability to communicate directly with the German emigrants in their own language, and thereby warn them of the activities of these persuasive rogues, was an evident advantage.

The March journal brought more interesting observations. On the 5th he wrote 'It is remarkable how many criminal refugees come through here on their way to America. One landlord told me that of every hundred lodgers he gets, he thinks he can safely say ninety are this class of people. Most of them go to America, a few to Australia to the diggings.' On such foundations were 'the gangs of New York', for example, to be built. His June journal is particularly informative on the difficulties he was encountering in his ministry to the very large number of German emigrants with whom he had to deal. 'There were days in April and May when at least a couple of thousand were in at a time, so much so that the newspapers noticed on several occasions these very large numbers that were seen at times roaming around in groups in different parts of Liverpool.' The clear implication is that the local people found such concentrations, with whom they could scarcely communicate, if at all, to be intimidating to say the least. Not that they were in Liverpool for long; Schmitz noted that most of the emigrants had come from Hamburg and Rotterdam, via Hull, and then 'conducted by their Agents to the different Lodging Houses.' Clearly the 'emigrant trade' from Germany was efficiently organised, However, Schmitz bewailed the lack of a German

Emigrant Depot, where these people could be housed together for the few days they were in Liverpool before boarding their ships, rather than scattered wherever lodgings could be found. These, he knew, were the ones who would most easily fall victim to the 'Runners' and to other enticements. As he had pointed out in his Journal for March, 1854: 'Few at home . . . on account of the fine weather and the races'.

Although assiduous in his ship visiting and tours of the lodging houses, Schmitz was not as convinced of the value of this as Welsh seems to have been. Lodging house keepers, perhaps because in some cases they were allied to the 'Runners', could be cool towards him, he observed. Ship visiting was not particularly rewarding, either. The German emigrants, who were his main concern, tended to be scattered among those from other nations, and, inevitably as a result, if they were Christians, came from different denominations and with differing ecclesial allegiance. The best he could do was provide the ships about to set sail with a 'goodly number' of tracts and books. Here he was supported by SPCK, by 'the Homily and Prayer Book Society, the Religious Tract Society and the Bible Society'. But Schmitz was a realist; 'They [i.e. the books and tracts] were well received, not because the Germans were particularly religious, but wanted something to read on the long voyages'. His German emigrants especially seemed to have confronted him with a greater degree of scepticism and indifference than the more mixed bag did Welsh. 'A considerable number amongst them do not believe in the immortality of the soul. Religion is therefore neglected . . . it is considered as something superannuated and which mainly seems to them does not answer as it were for this enlightened age.' For this situation he unequivocally blamed the complacency of the church in Germany. 'Is it therefore to be wondered at when we see the present political and social state of the Germans? The church in Germany must rouse from her lethargy and her Ministers must give full proof of their Ministry or indeed times will come which are awful to meditate upon'. The Imperial Germany of Kaiser William II or the Third Reich of Adolf Hitler were in 1854 a long way off, but the seed-bed of scepticism and indifference that Schmitz could detect all around him was, indeed, to bear a terrible harvest.

In their differing but complementary ways, the reports and journals of Welsh and Schmitz provide us with insights into the challenges of a now vanished ministry. That mass emigration posed a challenge to the institutional churches there can be no doubt, and SPG did its best to meet the need. The Established Church of England, with its settled parochial structure and legal framework, was in fact ill-equipped to meet the challenge, except by employing, through a voluntary society like SPG, clergy who ministered on the margins of those structures. Schmitz, in fact, highlighted one of the problems; the question of marriage. Evidently he was, at least from time to time, requested to solemnise marriages between emigrants. The rector of Liverpool was as accommodating as he could be, permitting Schmitz to officiate on such occasions in his church. That was not the problem; as Schmitz put it, 'the law required a stay of at least a fortnight in England, and very few could make it that long – even a week'. As we have seen, many emigrants were in Liverpool for only a matter of days before their ship sailed. Those who had, perhaps, met and fallen in love during their journeys from Hamburg or Rotterdam, and wished to marry and therefore not be placed in the allocated separate accommodation for men and women, were prevented from so doing by the rigidity of the law. Baptisms and celebrations of the Holy Communion, the provision of funerals, the Emigrant Chaplains could, and did provide, but all too often the desired marriage 'in the sight of God' had to be denied them. For a married man like Schmitz, or for Welsh, who was himself married during the course of his ministry to the emigrants, the reality of this disappointment must have weighed heavily upon them.

Notes

[1] I am grateful to the staff of the Weston Library, Bodleian Library, for their assistance; and to the Oxford Centre for Methodism and Church History, Oxford Brookes University, and in particular its Director, Professor William Gibson, for hospitality, facilitating the preparation of this paper.

[2] For this, and subsequent information in this paragraph, I am indebted to National Museums Liverpool, Maritime Archives & Library, Information Sheet 64, 'Liverpool and Emigration in the 19th and 20th Centuries'.

[3] The Information Sheet 64 does not specify which of the Scandinavian countries is included.

[4] Geoffrey Best, *Mid-Victorian Britain 1851–75* (London, 1979) p. 147.

[5] Information Sheet 64.

[6] Ibid.

[7] Ibid. By 1854 the Lodging Houses were being inspected, and had to be licensed.

[8] Bodleian Library, Oxford, SPG Archive, C/EMIGRANTS/1. Quarterly Report of the Revd J. W. Welsh, 12 February, 1855. References to this archive will subsequently be abbreviated to BLO/SPG/EM.

[9] St Aidan's had been founded in 1846, and under its first principal, the Revd Joseph Baylee, had a profoundly Evangelical ethos, though there is no evidence in Welsh's reports, despite

having been trained at the college, that he shared that emphasis to any great extent. Although Liverpool was by far the most significant port of embarkation, emigrants also travelled from others. SPG supported chaplains at Deptford, Southampton, Bristol & Gloucester, and Londonderry. The chaplain for Bristol & Gloucester, the Revd R. A. Taylor, worked in conjunction with the Revd J. Hollins, described as 'chaplain to the Boatmen' – presumably on the Kennet & Avon Canal. The Revd J. Higginbotham, chaplain at Londonderry, was part-time, serving also as curate at the Church of Ireland cathedral. There were also chaplains supported at some of the ports where the emigrants landed, for example, Sydney, Port Phillip, Adelaide, and Capetown.

[10] The Depot featured in the *Illustrated London News* for 10 July 1852.
[11] See Keith Pescod, *Good Food, Bright Fires and Civility. British Emigrant Depots of the Nineteenth Century* (Kew, Vic., Aus, 2001).
[12] BLO/SPG/EM/1. 12 November 1854.
[13] The first and second were those of 1832 and 1848. Norman Longmate, *King Cholera. The Biography of a Disease* (London, 1966) p. 181.
[14] Ibid., p. 195.
[15] Liverpool had been the first in the UK to appoint such an officer, in 1846.
[16] The population of Liverpool in 1854 was some 433,814, of whom 1,290 died in the cholera epidemic, i.e. 2.97 per 1000. Gerry Kearns, Paul Laxton & Joy Campbell, 'Duncan and the Cholera Test: Public Health in mid-Nineteenth Century Liverpool'. www.hslc.org.uk/wp-content/uploads/143-6-Kearns-Laxton-Campbell.pdf (accessed 13 September 2017).
[17] Longmate, op. cit., p. 98.
[18] Ibid., p. 99.
[19] BLO/SPG/EM/1 12 February 1855.
[20] BLO/SPG/EM/1 12 February, 1856.
[21] BLO/SPG/EM/1 12 May 1855.
[22] From the late 17th century onwards the East India Company had given passage to women as prospective brides for its officers in India – hence the designation of its vessels carrying them as 'the Fishing Fleet'. Anne de Courcy, *The Fishing Fleet. Husband Hunting in the Raj* (New York, 2014). Sailings were still under way in the 1850s, and, indeed, in de Courcy's phrase, covered 'the whole span of the Raj'. (p. 16).
[23] BLO/SPG/EM/1 12 August 1855.
[24] BLO/SPG/EM/1 12 November 1855.
[25] Presumably this can be accounted for, at least in part, by the discharge of men from military service at the end of the war.
[26] BLO/SPG/EM/1 12 May 1856.
[27] BLO/SPG/EM/1 12 August 1856.
[28] BLO/SPG/EM/1 12 August 1857.
[29] BLO/SPG/EM/1 12 February 1857.
[30] BLO/SPG/EM/1 12 November 1854.
[31] St Patrick's College, Maynooth, Co. Kildare, had been founded in 1795 as the National Seminary for the Catholic Church in Ireland. Numbers of seminarians had grown steadily, and by the 1850s Maynooth was the largest Catholic seminary in the world.
[32] BLO/SPG/EM/1 12 February 1858.
[33] BLO/SPG/EM/1 12 November 1855.
[34] Bill Jones, 'A wondrous gaol is the emigrant ship': Shipboard experiences of Welsh emigrants in the nineteenth century (Benllech, Aled Eames Memorial Lecture, 2014), especially pp. 22–3.

'The Country is on the Move'

35 Quoted by Bill Jones, art. cit, p. 22.
36 BLO/SPG/EM/1 12 February and 12 May 1857. The first missionaries of the Church of the Latter-Day Saints, the Mormons, had landed – in Liverpool – from the United States in 1837–41, and by 1850 some 7,500 converts had emigrated to the States, some aided by the church's Perpetual Emigration Fund, which had been established in 1849, grant-aiding passages for those who were to settle in Utah. At a modest rate of interest, the grants were repayable once the emigrant had settled and become established.
37 BLO/SPG/EM/1 12 February 1857.
38 BLO/SPG/EM/1 Folio 3, 1862.
39 James Barnett, 'Willich's Thirty-Second Indiana Volunteers' *http:/www.library.cincymuseum. org/topics/c/files/civilwar/chsbull-v57-n1-wil-049.pd/* (accessed 30 May 2019).
40 BLO/CEMIGRANTS/1, f 24, and for much of what follows.
41 Ibid.

'THE BIGGEST STINK IN THE WORLD': THOMAS SOUTHWOOD SMITH, SOCIAL CONSCIENCE, AND LONDON

Figure 4: Thomas Southwood Smith.
Portrait believed to be by his partner Margaret Gillies, in the possession of his descendants. Reproduced by permission.

In James Clavell's novel of the founding of the Crown Colony of Hong Kong in the middle years of the nineteenth century, *Tai-Pan*, there is a confrontation. It takes place between the principal character in the book, the merchant entrepreneur Dirk Struan and his son Colum, who has just arrived from Scotland with the news that Struan's immediate family, including his wife, has been all but wiped out by cholera. In a period of four months, many thousands had died. The confrontation between father and son is over the question of personal hygiene. The Chinese, says the father, 'think there's some connection between dung and disease', and he orders his incredulous son 'From now on, ashore or afloat – you bathe your whole body once a week. You use paper and wash your hands. You have your clothes washed once a week. You drink nae water, only tea. And you brush your teeth daily'. To Colum this is 'madness'; 'Just because of some heathen Chinese customs, I have to change my whole way of life!' His father remains inflexible, pointing out that his son has lice in his hair and stinks. The rejoinder from the still stubbornly protesting son is 'Best you go to London, Father. That's the biggest stink in the world. Lice are a curse of people, and that's the end of it. If people hear you go on about lice and stink, they'll think you mad.'[1]

The skill of the novelist is demonstrated here; the encapsulating of an argument within the space of less than two pages. I have quoted from Clavell's novel because the argument that he describes between the father and the son epitomises that which was going on at all levels of British society at the time. Was there, indeed, a connection between 'dung and disease'? It had little to do with class or intellect – something Clavell subtly reveals, for it is the father, who has raised himself from the humblest of origins (he had been a powder-monkey at the Battle of Trafalgar) who is open to what could be and were interpreted as new and strange ideas. It is the university-educated son who stubbornly adheres to received notions. This was the world which the physician and Unitarian minister Thomas Southwood Smith inhabited throughout his working life.

In the inaugural Octavia Hill Memorial Lecture at Wisbech, which I gave in 1993, the subject of which was Southwood Smith, Octavia's grandfather, I said 'It is clearly impossible to consider in any detail most of the multifarious activities of this man . . .' within the compass of a single paper.[2] That conclusion still holds good; indeed, it would be very difficult to do him justice within the covers of a single monograph. However, the outlines of his life and career, from his birth at Martock in Somerset in 1788 until his death, which occurred when visiting his younger daughter Emily in Florence in 1861, are sufficiently well documented to require no rehearsal.[3] This paper, rather, focuses on some aspects of his years of public service, in particular the period between 1830, when he was appointed to the staff of the London Fever Hospital, and 1854, when he was, in effect, forcibly retired; and on exploring how his contributions, especially to what has come to be known as 'the sanitary idea' were informed and to some extent driven forward by the theology that he espoused.

Over-specialisation is a besetting sin of historical research, and it is, perhaps, therefore not surprising that medical historians have tended to ignore, or at least down-play, Southwood Smith's theological and philosophical convictions, and ecclesiastical historians have taken little or no notice of him, because for most of his life he was primarily associated with, and identified with, matters scientific and medical. He himself recognised that there could be a tension or a conflict of interest between ordained ministry and medical practice for someone hoping to undertake both simultaneously. He had experienced it in himself in Edinburgh and in Yeovil, when attempting to pursue a dual career between 1813 and 1820, and in that latter year had opted to focus upon his medical practice, without, however, ever entirely abandoning the ministry. He continued thereafter to preach occasionally, until the latter years of his life, and was sometimes referred to as 'the Reverend Dr Southwood Smith'. It is not a surprise, therefore, that scholars have hitherto concentrated on what for some forty years was to be the dominant profession. However, arguably, those years would not have followed the course that they did had not philosophical and theological convictions formed earlier directed it.

What then, in essence, were those convictions? There are hints in Southwood Smith's little penny tract of 1824 *Unitarian Worship vindicated by the Precepts and Example of Jesus Christ*,[4] namely the necessity of daily prayer to Almighty God in obedience to the example and authority of Jesus Christ, with the Lord's Prayer as the pattern. Implicit in this simple tract –of only eight small pages– is that the fruit of such earnest prayer should be humility in ourselves ('forgive us our trespasses'), compassion for others ('as we forgive those who trespass against us'), and the recognition of the equality of all humanity before God, with the opportunity for all to live healthy and fulfilled lives ('give us – [all] – our daily bread'). There is no evidence that Southwood Smith ever departed from the exercise of these principles and precepts.

His ideas were most fully developed in what he always considered his most important publication, *Illustrations of the Divine Government*, which first appeared in 1816, and ran through four editions in the ensuing decade. The work, a distillation of lectures he had delivered in Edinburgh, openly espoused the doctrine of Universal Salvation (sometimes known as Universal Reconciliation) which argues that all people, no matter how evil they may be in the lives they live in this world, are created by God, and that eventually God will bring them all back to Himself. After death each person will be judged by God according to their deeds; there is punishment for evil-doing, according to God's desire for justice, but this punishment is temporary and not eternal. 'Eternal' as used in the phrase 'eternal punishment' is to be interpreted as meaning 'continuous for a time' and not 'continuous through eternity'. Eventually, in God's good time, everyone comes back to Him. God, however, will not compel anyone to turn to him. It is likely that Smith, who in adult life had a consistent repulsion for the rigid Calvinism of his upbringing, would have agreed with Charles Wesley here. Ernest Rattenbury expressed it thus: 'Man is a personality with a will that God will not – indeed, on account of man's constitution, cannot – break . . . From God's point of view everything has been done to save mankind that could be done . . . God will not compel men to obey Him. He offers grace, not a whip.'[5] Man could resist; in effect, choose not to be saved. The doctrine, as Jeremy White argued in 1712, was 'to represent God in his most amiable excellencies and vindicate the super-eminence of His love, which is His nature, and the full latitude of His mercy and goodness towards His creatures, which has had a cloud or veil of darkness drawn over it in the minds of the generality of mankind.'[6] For anyone who, like Southwood Smith, held firmly to this understanding of the lot of mankind, the way forward was clear. This is how he expressed it:

> The person who habitually contemplates all mankind as children of one common Father, and appointed to one common destiny, cannot be a persecutor or a bigot. He may see much error, which he may lament, and much misconduct, which he may pity; but a generous affection towards the whole human race will dilate his heart. To the utmost of his ability he will enlighten the ignorant, correct the erring, sustain the weak, bear with the prejudiced and reclaim the vicious. Firm to his own principles, he will not trench on the liberty of others. He will not harshly censure, or suspect an evil motive where integrity and conscience obviously direct the conduct. Mildness will be on his lips; forbearance will mark his actions; and universal charity will connect him with the wise and good of all climes, and of all religions.[7]

Affection for and compassion towards humankind without distinction, integrity, patience and forbearance, and a burning desire to educate and enlighten – to lift White's 'cloud and veil of darkness' – to improve the lot of the least advantaged, were the driving forces of the whole of Southwood Smith's public life and endeavours, and all grew out of this theological conviction.

Alongside the doctrine of Universal Salvation has to be placed, as Professor R. K. Webb rightly pointed out, that of Necessitarianism.[8]

This is a rather more difficult doctrine to understand and accept, but it was one that was espoused by many Unitarians in Southwood Smith's day. In its most extreme form, which Smith did not accept, just as he rejected an undiluted universalism; it denied freewill. It was, as Webb put it, 'a deterministic and generally materialistic philosophy... In this view actions are necessary consequences of motives formed in the mind by prior circumstances.' Southwood Smith's necessitarianism was more nuanced, what might be termed 'practical necessitarianism'; in his case, a vocation born out of a searingly painful personal circumstance. His own sustained interest in 'fever', its nature and cause, and thus his long years of labour at the London Fever Hospital, and his *Treatise on Fever*, published in 1830, can and arguably should be traced back to the premature death in 1812, after only four years of marriage, of his beloved first wife, Anne Read, from 'fever', a loss from which he never fully recovered.

In addition, Smith was convinced that sin and suffering result from disobedience to divinely established and discoverable law. Education here was the key, knowledge and understanding the consequence, which together enabled the discovery of the divine law, and thus the overcoming of suffering and the combatting of sin. There was no question of unrestricted choice; the Christian, in Smith's definition of the term, had to act. His aim and object would be, as he put it, 'to extend the knowledge, to mitigate the suffering, and to increase the happiness of mankind.' He concluded 'Without doubt this is the great business of life; whoever succeeds in it most, is the wisest, the ablest, and the happiest of his race; and even he whose measure of success is not great, cannot be without satisfaction, so long as he is conscious of the wish and the effort to accomplish more.'[9] There is an echo here of William Blake, a poet to whom Smith was devoted:

> I will not cease from Mental Fight
> Nor shall my Sword sleep in my hand
> Till we have built Jerusalem
> In England's green and pleasant land.

It is against this background that Smith's work at the London Fever Hospital; on the Royal Commission on the employment of children (1833); in the compiling for the Poor Law Commission between 1838 and 1839 of his report on the sanitary conditions of Bethnal Green and Whitechapel; and that on the employment of women and children underground in the mining industry (1842–3); has to be judged. His great facility as a writer and his years of experience as a lecturer and preacher meant that, as Professor Webb has said, 'he was superb in creating and moulding public and political opinion' and galvanising people into action. His eirenic temperament enabled him to work constructively with men and women with whom he had, personally, very little in common, and though, no doubt in private deeply hurt by the jibes and criticisms that were from time to time aimed at him, it was not in his nature to respond in kind. As a result the verdict of history, such as it is, has not always been fair or balanced.

II

Smith's concern with 'fever' was, as noted earlier, to occupy a prominent place in his medical life, if indeed, it was not his primary work. The London Fever Hospital had been founded in 1802, and in 1849 moved to impressive new buildings in Liverpool Road, Islington, which still survive, though no longer serving their original purpose.[10] In 1849, when the hospital was about to move into its new accommodation, the director, W. H. O. Sankey, expressed a wish that wards in the new building should be appropriated 'for our share of children's diseases.' Prominent among the supporters of the idea, if, indeed, he hadn't suggested it in the first place, was Southwood Smith. In this advocacy he was joined by the Unitarian novelist Elizabeth Gaskell, his colleagues the Earl of Shaftesbury, Lord Morpeth and Edwin Chadwick, the philanthropist Angela Burdett Coutts, and his friend the novelist Charles Dickens.[11] As Sankey told the pioneer paediatrician, Charles West, in 1850, the idea was 'strenuously opposed' by one of the medical staff, unnamed, but possibly Alexander Tweedie, and the initiative stalled. It was not, however, abandoned or forgotten. From it were to grow the endeavours to found what was to become in 1852 the Great Ormond Street Hospital, the first institution in the English-speaking world to be solely dedicated to the care of sick children. On 21 January 1852 the General Board of Health gave its official sanction for the opening of the hospital, which took place, rather appropriately, on St Valentine's Day, and that document was signed by Southwood Smith and Edwin Chadwick.[12] Smith's passionate concern for the welfare of children had already been amply demonstrated by his work on the two Royal Commissions referred to above, and exemplified in his own family life, so his promotion and support for hospital provision specifically for children is not at all surprising. *En passant*, it is worth noting that many of those who supported the initiative from 1849 onwards were among his own personal friends and colleagues. Sankey may have been the man who publicly floated the idea, but it cannot be doubted that the energetic 'behind-the-scenes' lobbying for it was the work of Southwood Smith.

Smith's first formal association with the London Fever Hospital was in 1829, when his name appears on the list of subscribers (at one guinea, which entitled him to be a governor). The following year he was elected as the Second Physician, the first being Alexander Tweedie, who had been Senior Physician since 1824. Tweedie was an Edinburgh Scot, whose first career had been as a surgeon, but, unusually, he had migrated to medicine, qualifying L.R.C.P. in 1822 and F.R.C.P. in 1838. The duties of the physicians were laid down by the hospital's management; one of them had to visit the wards daily and keep accurate registers of patients and the remedies employed. An incomplete set of Patients' Registers survives from 1824, some of the entries being in Smith's characteristic, rather sprawling, handwriting. Professor William Bynum, who examined them, commented 'The volumes' tersely recorded histories and physical examinations remind us that eighteenth and early nineteenth centuries diagnoses of fever do not conform to any single modern diagnostic category.'[13] Indeed, differential diagnosis was then in its infancy; as Bynum remarks, 'During our period fever was a disease in itself, rather than simply a sign of disease.'[14] Much of the argument – and here we find ourselves back with Clavell's novel – was concerned with discovering the 'cause' of fever, and its prevention, but, as Bynum points out, Smith, though fully sharing in this concern, 'never lost his faith in the curative powers of medicine.'[15]

III

Tweedie and Smith were to work together for some thirty years, the latter succeeding the former as senior physician in 1860, only a year before his death. Yet their views on fever were very different. Tweedie, as his *Clinical Illustrations of Fever* (1828) reveals, was a contagionist; Smith was not. For the contagionist, fever was caused by an as yet unidentified germ, and therefore infectious; it could be transmitted from person to person. That was convincing, as far as it went. The weakness of the argument lay in the definition of 'fever' as a disease, as noted above, and not as a symptom of a variety of diseases. Later, once secure differential diagnoses had become established, then it was possible to discriminate between some 'fevers' which were infectious and others which were not, and treat them accordingly. Tweedie, and the others who supported his views, were partially right, but largely for the wrong reasons.

Southwood Smith, on the other hand, was what would have been called a 'miasmatist', but which today is more often referred to as a 'localist', but in a limited and specialist sense which distanced him significantly from more ardent advocates of that viewpoint. In essence, miasmatists were those who believed that 'fever' was transmitted by polluted air; infinitesimally small particles formed a miasma from rotten and decaying matter and material, and these contaminated and infected those who inhaled them. Thus the attack on 'stink', and the drive to remove rotten and faecal matter – the emphasis upon hygiene– which formed the basis of the 'sanitary idea'.

In 1854, during the cholera epidemic which so afflicted London, Southwood Smith published a pamphlet, *Results of Sanitary Improvement*, which had a wide circulation.[16] In this work, written as he says, when 'the new and terrible plague of modern times is again amongst us,'[17] he reiterated the conviction that he had held for many years that there had to be 'the enforcement of all practical means of cleansing, and the resolute removal of nuisances', so that the worst effects of the disease could be warded off.[18] Thus far he was allied with the localists. However, in his view, this did not go far enough. Back in 1830, in his *Treatise on Fever*, he had criticised the advocates of localism for a tendency to mistake secondary and primary phenomena.[19] The removal of 'nuisances' did at least limit the spread of diseases such as cholera, he agreed, and cited examples from Newcastle, and Baltimore in the United States, where prompt action along these lines had had the desired effect. But the primary cause remained; if the problem was to be attacked at source, then the primary cause was to be found elsewhere.

The answer for Smith was an obvious one; there was an urgent necessity to remove 'the degrading influence of the present dwellings of the labouring classes', and substitute housing that met five criteria: 1. The thorough subsoil drainage of the site; 2. The free admission of air and light to every inhabited room; 3. The abolition of the cesspool and the substitution of the water-closet, involving complete house drainage;

4. An abundant supply of pure water; and 5. Means for the immediate removal of all solid house refuse not capable of suspension in water, and of being carried off by water.[20] Such dwellings, he had long advocated, and through the Health of Towns Association and other related societies, such as the Metropolitan Association for Improving the Dwellings of the Industrious Classes, had worked to provide. Only when there was the widespread adoption of what would later become known as 'slum clearance' would it be possible to effect the necessary improvements in social, moral and health conditions of those who were the most vulnerable in society. As Smith put it, 'When the house ceases to be a sty, and possesses the conditions which render it capable of being made a home, then, but not till then, may it receive, with some hope of benefit, the schoolmaster and the minister of religion.'[21] Cleanliness had to come before Godliness. Sweeping out devils was not enough; the house that harboured them had to be rebuilt. Attitudes had to be changed and old ways and habits abandoned; once again we are back to the confrontation between father and son in Clavell's *Tai-Pan*.

Probably no one in England knew more about the close relationship between environment and disease than Southwood Smith. Yet, like everyone else, he remained at a disadvantage. Although the argument raged between contagionists and miasmatists, because of the prevailing understanding of 'fever', and ignorance as to the cause of epidemic diseases such as cholera, then no totally convincing argument would be advanced to support either position. Both, in fact, had some inkling of the truth, but both were operating at the limit of knowledge and understanding. Smith's understanding was, in fact, to lead him to concur in what was to be, without exaggeration, a medical and social disaster.

As early as 1824 Smith had, through his friendship with the Utilitarian philosopher Jeremy Bentham, become acquainted with the young lawyer Edwin Chadwick, who in 1830 became Bentham's secretary. The two men, Chadwick and Smith, were as different as chalk and cheese, and yet their subsequent working lives were to be constantly intertwined. Smith, amiable, eirenic, sociable, devout, cultured and approachable; Chadwick, who in contrast had what Peter Mandler called 'a passion for the "quick fix" technical or administrative solution to deep-seated social problems',[22] was anti-populist, anti-democratic, perfervid, prickly, lacking in social skills or sense of humour, distant and aloof. Chadwick came to epitomise the soulless, utilitarian bureaucrat, addicted to regulation and inflexible administrative procedures, but he was a hard worker, an assiduous collector of data, and an administrator bordering on genius. In 1832 he had worked effectively on the Royal Commission on the Poor Laws; the following year on that on the Employment of Children in Factories.

In 1838 he was turning his attention to public health and sanitation, and in 1842, drawing on his own and Southwood Smith's experience, produced 'one of the most celebrated (and best-selling) of all Victorian blue-books, the *Report on the Sanitary Condition of the Labouring Population of Great Britain*.[23] He was, therefore, despite his public and private persona, the obvious choice in 1848 to head the first national public health authority, the General Board of Health, under the presidency of Lord Morpeth. At first he was the only paid commissioner; his colleague (unpaid) was Lord Ashley, later the social reformer the 7th Earl of Shaftesbury. In 1849 they were joined, in a voluntary capacity, by the only medically qualified commissioner, Southwood Smith. He became in effect, though not in name, England's first 'Chief Medical Officer'. Given the shortcomings of the legislation under which the General Board of Health had been set up, the only way in which Smith could be paid – his salary was £1,200 a year, a not inconsiderable sum, was by appointing him a commissioner under the provisions of the Metropolitan Interments Act.[24] His appointment was not universally welcomed by the medical profession, the campaigning journal *The Lancet* being particularly hostile. *The Lancet* did not doubt his competence, but feared that under the terms of his appointment a physician would be subordinate to others unqualified in medicine. In some quarters his appointment under the Interments Act was regarded as a joke in rather doubtful taste. One Dr Henry Rumsey commented, 'Who would have thought that in the last decade of advancing civilisation and in a nation boasting of its intellectual and material resource, of its administrative energy and efficiency, the whimsical experiment should have actually been tried of appointing three non-medical authorities –two Lords and a Barrister [i.e. Lords Morpeth and Ashley, and Chadwick] to preserve the health of the living; and then, after a year or so of doubtful success, calling in a Physician [Smith] to bury the dead'.[25]

Almost immediately following its formation, the Board faced its first major test, the return of epidemic cholera, the disease which had ravaged the country in 1832. At its very first meeting, the outbreak of cholera in the port of Hull was reported to the members. The spread of the disease was rapid and serious, and the Board had no coercive powers to order local authorities to act along the lines they advocated. As Brundage put it, 'the Board could do little but urge and cajole,'[26] and Smith's circular laying down guidelines for action was so overtly 'miasmatic' – and thus would involve the local authorities in expense – that it was fiercely resented and resisted in many quarters. In the spring of 1849, as the weather warmed up, the death-toll mounted. 35,000 died, 15,000 in London alone. Sadly, this astonishingly high figure for the capital cannot be accounted for solely by the virulence of the disease. Wearing his hat as a commissioner on the Metropolitan Commission of Sewers, Edwin Chadwick, at the height of the epidemic, insisted on the flushing of all 'miasmatic' deposits into the Thames. There can be little doubt that his fellow-member of the General Board of Health, Lord Ashley, and Southwood Smith, concurred with Chadwick's decision, even if they were not directly involved in the making of it. The result was disastrous.

Many Londoners still drew their drinking water directly from the river. Ignorant of, or at least resistant to, the fact that cholera was a waterborne disease, the decision contributed to the excruciatingly painful deaths of many, possibly even thousands, of the city's inhabitants. The decision pre-dated the Metropolitan Water Supply Act if 1852, but this itself relied on the advice of three chemists who asserted that where organic contamination was concerned 'the indefinite dilution of such matters in the vast volume of the well-aerated stream is likely to lead to their destruction by oxidation, and to cause their disappearance.'[27] The Act did not therefore order the removal of the source of London water to areas far away from the source of contamination. To be fair to Chadwick and the framers of the 1852 Act, there was no understanding at that time that the cholera 'comma' bacillus existed, was transmitted by water, and was not 'soluble' in it.[28] Chadwick's decision has been likened, with rather unpardonable hyperbole, to an act of terrorism. In his review of Steven Johnson's *The Ghost Map: The Story of London's Terrifying Epidemic – and How it Changed Science, Cities and the Modern World*, Aaron Carver highlighted Johnson's verdict that 'a 21st century biological terrorist couldn't have devised a more ingenious plot to endanger the city's population.'[29] This is, of course, totally unfair to Chadwick and his advisers; it takes no account of either knowledge or motivation. The '21st century biological terrorist' would be acting in full knowledge of the consequences, and the motive of his action would be destructive and not, as Chadwick hoped and believed, at the least palliative.

The causative organism of cholera, the water-borne 'comma' bacillus, was not identified by Robert Koch until 1882, and although there was, by 1849, some medical scientists, such as John Snow, who suspected that there was a link between polluted water and the epidemic spread of cholera, this was still a theory and not an established fact. Snow's *On the Mode of Communication of Cholera* was first published in 1849, the year of the epidemic outbreak, it at first received little notice or attention. It was certainly not accepted by the members of the General Board of Health. The second edition of 1855, which contained the statistical evidence which he had compiled during the 1854 outbreak, still made little impact on received opinion, and it was not until the end of the century, long after his death, that the accuracy of his observations was generally accepted. Lord Morpeth, the president of the General Board of Health, Lord Ashley, Southwood Smith and Chadwick, in summary, cannot be made to shoulder the blame for a decision made in good faith, even though the results were tragic.[30]

IV

In 1854, as Webb observed, 'the General Board of Health fell victim to inadequate design, narrow medical doctrine, mounting reaction against centralised government, and resentment of Chadick's high-handedness'.[31] The Board was dissolved, and neither Chadwick, then aged 54, nor Smith, 66, ever again held public appointments. Vindictiveness as well as bureaucratic inflexibility may well have played a part in the denial to Southwood Smith of a pension, on the ground that he had had only four years of paid employment. Despite being reduced to penury –his position at the London Fever Hospital was honorary, and in 1850 on joining the Board in a salaried capacity, he had relinquished the last of his private practice– with characteristic modesty and fortitude he did not protest. It was left to his friends to rally round; a public subscription was raised, and, belatedly, and it is to be suspected grudgingly, as a result the authorities relented and he was given a pension of £300.

Mention has been made earlier in this paper of Smith's friendship with the novelist Charles Dickens, with particular reference to the London Fever Hospital and the foundation of the Great Ormond Street Children's Hospital in 1852. That friendship dated back to the 1830s, and they remained frequent correspondents. Smith sent Dickens advance copies of his Royal Commission reports, and it was that of 1842, in particular, on the employment of women and children in the mines, which struck a chord with Dickens. In fact, in the June of 1841, when Smith was gathering the evidence for that report, he suggested to Dickens an expedition so that he could see for himself the conditions under which children laboured in coal mines.[32] Dickens was not free to undertake the visit at that time, but the following year, with Smith's support, he descended several Cornish tin mines.[33] Early in 1843 Smith sent Dickens an advance copy of his final report; its findings, Dickens said in acknowledgement, gave him great pain. Early in March he sent a message to Smith begging him to call to discuss the possibility of his writing a cheap pamphlet, provisionally entitled *An Appeal to the People of England, on behalf of the Poor Man's Child*. The ensuing discussion evidently gave him second thoughts, for on the 16 March he wrote again to Southwood Smith, saying that he was now thinking of relating his appeal to the Christmas season, and this would provide 'a sledge hammer [to] come down with twenty times the force – 20,000 times the force – I could exert by following my first idea.' The result of the second thoughts was the never-to-be surpassed *Christmas Carol*, published on 19 December of that year. Here is to be found that galaxy of memorable characters, Ebenezer Scrooge, Marley's ghost, the ghosts of Christmas past, present and to come, Tiny Tim, and the flying visit to the Cornish miners –the 1842 visit bearing fruit – along with the dire warning in Stave III, the children 'Ignorance' and 'Want', both representing situations Southwood Smith was striving to combat. *Christmas Carol* was written for Smith.[34] It did not, and does not, stand alone, for *The Chimes*, the following year's Christmas story, was another of Dickens's 'sledgehammer blows', this time against selfishness, complacency, materialism and greed.[35]

Evidence garnered by Smith also surfaced in, for example, *Oliver Twist*, *Dombey and Son*, and, most memorably of all, in *Bleak House*, where the character of physician Dr Woodcourt gives evidence of so many similarities with the novelist's friend. Only Smith's death in 1861 brought the friendship of the physician and the novelist to an end. After his enforced retirement in 1854, though he retained his honorary position at the London Fever Hospital, Smith, accompanied by his companion and partner of more than twenty years, the artist Margaret Gillies, left London to live in virtual retirement at Weybridge in Surrey. There in 1858 they were joined by Smith's second wife, from whom he had been estranged for some thirty years, and in that rather unconventional *menage a trois* he lived out the remainder if his life, dying on 10 December 1861 at the home of Emily, his younger daughter by his first wife, in Florence, where he had gone to convalesce from an illness. He is buried there, in the Protestant Cemetery, close to the grave of another famous Londoner who was one of his friends, Elizabeth Barrett Browning.

Notes

1. James Clavell, *Tai-Pan* (London, 1967) pp. 213-14.
2. John R. Guy, *Compassion and the art of the possible. Dr Southwood Smith as social reformer and public health pioneer* (Wisbech, The Octavia Hill Society, 1994) p. 4.
3. See especially his granddaughter's memoir, Mrs C L Lewes, *Dr Southwood Smith: a retrospect* (1898); the important article by F. N. L. Poynter, 'Thomas Southwood Smith – the man (1788-1861), *Proceedings of the Royal Society of Medicine*, 55 (1962) pp. 381-92, which did much to rescue him from obscurity; R. K. Webb, 'Southwood Smith: the intellectual sources of public service' in Dorothy & Roy Porter (eds), *Doctors, politics and society: historical essays* (1993) pp. 46-80, a valuable study of his thought and its context; my 1993 lecture (reprinted 1996) referred to above; and my subsequent papers, 'The Man who Isn't There (but Nearly Always Was)', *Acorn. Journal of the Octavia Hill Society*, 3, 2005-6, pp. 97-127; and 'The Use of the Dead to the Living. Jeremy Bentham, Thomas Southwood Smith, Happiness, and Dissection' in Peter Mitchell (ed.), *The Nature and Culture of the Human Body* (Lampeter, *Trivium*, 37, 2007, pp. 45-64.
4. Published by the Somerset and Dorset Unitarian Association, and 'printed for R. Hall, Library, Taunton'.
5. J. Ernest Rattenbury, *The Evangelical Doctrine of Charles Wesley's Hymns* (London, 2nd impression, 1942) pp. 129-30.
6. Jeremy White, *The Restoration of All Things; or a Vindication of the Graces and Goodness of God to be manifested at last in the Recovery of his whole Creation, out of their Fall* (London, 1712), quoted by Smith, *Divine Government*, p. 436.
7. Ibid., p. 430.
8. R. K. Webb, 'Thomas Southwood Smith, 1788-1861', *Oxford Dictionary of National Biography*.
9. Smith, *Divine Government*, Advertisement to the Third Edition, March, 1822.
10. The title page of *The Thirty-Ninth Report of the London Fever Hospital, Pancras Road, 1841* includes an engraving of the hospital as Southwood Smith first knew it. *The Forty-Seventh Report* (1849) contains a superb engraving, based on a 'bird's-eye-view' drawing by the architect, C. Fowler, of the new hospital, then about to open.
11. Jules Kosky, *Mutual Friends. Charles Dickens and Great Ormond Street Children's Hospital* (London, 1989) pp. 111, 14 and 78.
12. Ibid., p. 158.
13. W. F. Bynum, 'Hospital, Disease and Community: The London Fever Hospital 1801-1950' in Charles E. Rosenberg (ed.), *Healing and History* (New York, 1979) pp. 97-115 at p. 99. The history of the hospital was written in 1861 by Charles Dickens – one of his least-known publications – and first appeared in his journal *All the Year Round* in August, 1861. There can be little doubt that in writing this piece Dickens was responding to a request from his friend Southwood Smith, then senior physician at the hospital, as it is really an appeal for funding and support. As Smith died four months after its appearance, it was probably his last act of service to the hospital.

14 Bynum, op. cit., p. 99.
15 Ibid., p. 109.
16 At least 11,000 copies were printed by Charles Knight of Fleet Street on behalf of the General Board of Health and the Poor Law Board.
17 Ibid., p. 17.
18 Ibid., p. 18.
19 Margaret Pelling explored this in her *Cholera, Fever and English Medicine 1825-1865* (Oxford, 1978).
20 Ibid., pp. 21 and 4. Ironically, it was not only the dwellings of the poor which so often failed to meet the five criteria Smith laid down. The premature death of his supporter, Prince Albert, the Prince Consort, in 1861, from what is believed to be typhoid fever, has been attributed to the defective drains of Windsor Castle.
21 Smith, *Sanitary Improvement*, p. 22.
22 http://www.oxforddnb.com/view/printable/4013 (accessed 3 December 2009). The literature on Chadwick is vast. Among relevant works, see Benjamin Ward Richardson, *The Health of Nations. A review of the Works of Edwin Chadwick* (London, 2 vols, 1887); R. A. Lewis, *Edwin Chadwick and the Public Health Movement 1832-1854* (London, 1952); S. E. Finer, *The life and times of Sir Edwin Chadwick* (1952); Anthony Brindage, *England's 'Prussian Minister', Edwin Chadwick and the Politics of Government Growth 1832-1854* (University Park, Pa., 1988); Charles Webster, *The Victorian Public Health Legacy. A Challenge to the Future* (The Public Health Alliance, 1990); and Christopher Hamlin, 'Edwin Chadwick, "Mutton Medicine", and the Fever Question', *Bulletin of the History of Medicine*, 70 (1996), pp. 233-65. The concentration on Chadwick has all but relegated Southwood Smith's contribution to the 'Sanitary Idea' to oblivion.
23 Mandler, art. cit.
24 *Illustrated London News*, 17 August 1850, p. 131, column 1.
25 Quoted by W. M. Frazer, *A History of Public Health 1834-1939* (London, 1950) p. 48. In fairness to Smith, he had been acting as an unofficial as well as unpaid commissioner before his formal appointment. The accolade of 'England's First Chief Medical Officer' is usually awarded to Sir John Simon, who filled the office with great distinction from 1855, but in many ways the trail had been blazed, and the groundwork and scope of the work laid down, by Southwood Smith in the immediately previous years.
26 Brundage, op. cit., p. 135.
27 *Report on the Quality of the Supply of Water to the Metropolis* (BPP, 1851), XXIII, pp. 9-10.
28 See Anne Hardy, 'Water and the search for public health in London', *Medical History*, 28, no. 3 (1984) at p. 265.
29 http://www.inthesetimes.com/article/2942/choler_and_the_city/ (accessed 1 December 2099). Both the review, and the book reviewed, have to be treated with caution.
30 R. K. Webb, http://www.oxforddnb.com/articles/25/25917-article-html?back= (accessed 18 November 2009).
31 Ibid.
32 Madeline House and Graham Storey (eds), *The Letters of Charles Dickens, Vol. 2, 1840-1841* (Oxford, 1969) p. 290.
33 Madeline House, Graham Storey and Kathleen Tillotson (eds), *The Letters of Charles Dickens, Vol. 3, 1842-1843* (Oxford, 1974) p. 356 and n.5.
34 Ibid., pp. 435-6, 459-60, 461.
35 Edgar Johnson, *Charles Dickens. His Tragedy and Triumph* (London, rev. edn 1977) p. 250.

THE SEARCH FOR THE IDEAL MALE: THE ART OF HUGH EASTON

I

'Genius is intensity'. That remark, attributed to the French nineteenth century novelist Honoré de Balzac appears in a newspaper clipping pasted into a scrapbook held at the Victoria & Albert Museum Archive of Art and Design. Close to it is another quotation, this time anonymous, 'Drawing is at bottom, like all the arts, a kind of gesture, a method of dancing on paper.'[1] Intense; a dancer on paper – or in his case, on glass; each could be a description of the compiler of the scrapbook, the artist with whom this paper is primarily concerned, Hugh Easton.[2]

Easton was born in 1906, the son of a doctor, and was educated at Wellington College and the University of Tours. He originally determined to be a painter, and to that end studied in Italy and in Paris, but during that period was increasingly attracted to the designing of stained glass. Much to his father's consternation, he threw up his studies in France, and returned home to the firm of Blacking in Guildford, where under the guidance of the distinguished architect and designer, Sir Ninian Comper (a lifelong influence),[3] his pupil and assistant Christopher Webb (who became a personal friend), and Frederick Eden, who had studied under and worked with both William Butterfield and G. F. Bodley, he completed his training as a stained-glass artist.[4] Hugh's first studio was in Cambridge, but after World War II he settled in Hampstead, with his studio at Harpenden in Hertfordshire. Here Robert Hendra and Geoffrey Harper as painters, and T. G. and Denis Harris as cutters and glazier, turned Easton's designs into windows. Easton described his working method as starting with 'the roughest of small drawings', from which he developed a definitive cartoon. This was then passed on to Hendra and Harper for painting and interpreting, and to the two Harris's for fabrication. Easton does not seem to have personally involved himself in these latter stages of the creative process.[5]

This sense of 'distance' is important for any attempt to understand Hugh Easton. In his father's correspondence file, compiled after Hugh's death in August 1965 several writers refer to an elusive strand in the artist's personality. 'I think it was part of the very necessary protection of his life to keep many of his worlds separate' is the penetrating insight of one correspondent.[6] One side of him was gregarious; Peter Ryall, an employee at the Harpenden studio, described him as 'approachable and very friendly',[7] and his obituarist in the *City of London Squadron Magazine* referred to his 'gaiety and sense of fun.'[8] Edward Halliday, Chairman of the Artists' General Benevolent Institution, recalled an 'endearing personality',[9] and Peter Karnley, Vicar of Embleton, said of him 'Hugh always stood for me as an example of what the Bible means by *life* –life as opposed to mere existence, which is all so many people seem to reach.'[10]

Certainly he had a flamboyant side, driving an ostentatious Rolls-Royce, a member of Brooks's and the Fox Club (an exclusive dining club named in memory of the extrovert and extravagant eighteenth century Whig politician, Charles James Fox), and, as his diaries reveal, he was someone who enjoyed wining and dining with friends. To such friends he was readily accessible, and correspondents recalled 'the number of people who have come to him for help or to spill out troubles and never been turned away.'[11] In such he inspired real affection; the rector of Therfield in Hertfordshire, writing to him in March 1933 after one of Hugh's characteristically 'flying' visits, called him 'Very dear man ... it has greatly refreshed me to have had sight and sound of you.'[12]

But there was another side to him. Working through his archive, one is struck by how few photographs there are of him among his papers. One of them shows him in profile and in the shadows, with the large cartoon of the nurse for his Westminster Abbey window. From 'public' occasions, such as the unveiling of one of his stained-glass windows, he seems to have absented himself, and his diaries give very little insight into his intimate private life (some have pages torn out).[13] Indeed, there is a hint, in a letter dated October 1948 from Benedict Wailes, Prior of St Hugh's Charterhouse, Horsham, that Easton may have at one time considered joining the Carthusians, one of the Catholic Church's strictest orders of contemplatives.[14]

One cannot but be struck by the similarity between Easton and his contemporary Ian Fleming (of 'James Bond' fame).[15] Both during World War II served in the Royal Navy, mainly at the Admiralty, Fleming in the Naval Intelligence Division with the rank of Commander, and Easton as Naval Adviser to the Censorship Division of the Ministry of Information, with the same rank. Both exhibited the same complex personality, with an image at variance with reality – at home and relaxed within a defined circle of friends, but uneasy in, and eschewing where possible, wider company and the limelight. Both really lived through their art; Fleming in one sense through his literary creation James Bond (who, like himself, held the rank of Commander in the Royal Navy), arguably the man he wanted to be, and Easton through the pencil and brush of the visual artist. Both men, perhaps, could be said to be searching for the Ideal Male. And here the insight of the pioneering German sociologist Max Weber (1864–1920) is of some help; Weber was himself concerned with the 'ideal type', by 'ideal' meaning 'simply not exemplified in reality'.[16] It can be argued that Fleming's creation James Bond is a charismatic figure, and charisma is certainly something many of Easton's figures possess, again as Weber (who had been brought up in a strict Christian household, and fully understood the theological basis of the concept) saw as 'not part of the natural order; not part of the material world or the world of society. It comes from without'.[17] James Bond I leave to the literary critics and aficionados of espionage stories; it is with Easton's search that this paper is concerned, and having briefly considered the man himself, to that subject we must now turn.

II

Easton's diary "No.179" for 1936–7,[18] begins not with notes or appointments, but with pages of quick sketches of nude male and female figures, with the former predominant. Such sketches recur throughout the diary, primarily articulations of legs, buttocks and arms, the artist trying out all kinds of poses. They are quick sketches, in a way doodles; Easton 'dancing on paper', drawn from memory and the imagination rather than from life, and probably created whilst he was waiting for a train, or for his lunch to be served in a pub or restaurant.[19] The same kind of small sketches occur elsewhere, for example in the next diary, "No.180" for May–July 1937.[20] Easton was, therefore, in common with very many artists, a compulsive creator, and he was drawn, not at all surprisingly, to the unclothed human form.

His artistic training had been traditional. As Michael Jacobs has observed, 'before being allowed to copy from the model, the inexperienced artist would be expected to copy meticulously from casts or engravings of antique sculpture. When he came to the naked body itself, he was thus influenced by classical precedent, which would be re-inforced by the pose chosen for the model . . .'[21] Jacobs reminds his readers that [in] antiquity . . .' nudity was a natural part of life,[22] and Beatrice Farwell has pointed out that 'the Greeks had idolized and idealized the male nude in art rather more than the female.'[23]

'The male nude', Margaret Walters wrote in her authoritative study, 'is a forgotten subject . . . yet for nearly two thousand years the male nude overshadowed the female; the naked Gods and athletes of the ancient world, Christ stripped and suffering on the cross, Michelangelo's sensuous but spiritual nudes. In the two formative periods of Western art, early classical Greece and the early Italian Renaissance, the male body was all-important.'[24] The nude male figure after the Renaissance remained fundamental to art training until well into the twentieth century.[25] Throughout the centuries, therefore, the student artist was constantly reminded that the male body was the central image, sensual and ideal, in classical Greek art.

It was an art which emphasised masculine beauty, with close attention to detail. Here is to be found the epitome of the heroic, the athletic, of what Walters called 'ideal, godlike detachment.'[26] The Strangford Apollo of the Fifth Century BC, at the British Museum, the 'Athlete', after Polykleitos of circa 430 BC at the National Museum in Athens, and Praxiteles' 'Hermes with the Baby Dionysus' of at least a century later, now in the Olympia Museum in Greece, all depict the ideal against which all other human types were to be judged. The European Renaissance rejoiced in the rediscovery of such works, and the ideals they embodied, as Michelangelo's 'David' in Florence, dating from the first years of the sixteenth century, or his amazing drawing of the 'Risen Christ', now in the Royal Library at Windsor Castle, so unmistakeably remind us.[27]

Hugh Easton was only one of countless artists who have stood in this tradition. The heroic and the athletic fascinated and appealed strongly to him, as his scrapbook so clearly reveals.[28] He was drawn to those who exemplified for him virtue, manliness, virility. Thus inserted into its pages as are newspaper photographs of Guy Gibson, VC, of 'Dam Busters' fame, and also of the German Field Marshals Rommel and von Rundstedt. What might be called the 'heroic dead' of his own time, especially those who died in wartime operations, he found especially attractive; Flight Lieutenant Richard Hope Hillary, a Spitfire pilot, killed at the age of 23, and Lieutenant B. A. Ludford-Astley, killed aged 22.

Here are the men who for Easton epitomised the young, handsome, indeed the 'classical' hero; these are the men who, to the author's father's generation in the Forces, were the 'Brylcreem Boys',[29] emulated and imitated by those in uniform and 'civvy street' alike.

In 1949, Easton was called upon to design a memorial window for the main hall of Rolls-Royce's Derby factory, where so many of the engines which powered the planes whose pilots had fought and won the Battle of Britain had been manufactured. The window inspired a poem written by Frederick Archer, a sheet-metal worker at the plant before, during, and after the war years. Archer caught perfectly Easton's intention:

> Enshrined here, that clear eyed, clean limbed boy
> Embodies all the greatness of our race
> Devoted duty, Selfless sacrifice
> Even to die with dignity and grace
> Alas! To drink so young the bitter gall
> Forsaking flowery paths at trumpet call.[30]

Here is the 'ideal male', and he is replicated in many of Easton's stained-glass windows, not just in figures such as this one at Derby, or that of the kneeling American airman in his USAAF Memorial at Elvedon, but especially in his depictions of the person of Jesus Christ and of the warrior saints Michael and George.[31]

III

As a prelude to this, however, it is necessary to say something of the imaging of the person of Jesus Christ in Renaissance and later art, to better contextualise Easton's work. Christ to the Christian is God incarnate; He is both God and man. The mystery of the incarnation is the central truth of Christianity, and that truth, as John O'Malley pointed out, was re-emphasised in the theology of the Renaissance, and that theology's visual expression.[32] The Son of God is incarnated in the womb of the Virgin Mary, and that incarnation was manifested – revealed – when, as Fr O'Malley says, 'at his birth [he is] held in his mother's arms, shown to the Magi for their adoration, and most unmistakeably of all when [he] is subjected to the rite of circumcision.'[33] Here, in infancy, for the first time is revealed the naked Christ.[34]

In adult life the New Testament gospel texts make only two direct references to an unclothed Christ,[35] in John 13: 4, when at His last supper with His disciples, He 'laid aside his garments' before wrapping a towel about Himself, and washing His disciples' feet; and, as all four gospels record, immediately before His subsequent crucifixion, He was stripped of His clothing. The Jesus who hung on Calvary's cross did so naked, as one anonymous Florentine artist was to depict in the fifteenth century, and the English Catholic artist Eric Gill was also to show in the twentieth.[36] For Gill, as he said himself, 'the Incarnation was God's seal upon the goodness of the body . . .'[37] Indeed, that body, on Calvary brutally revealed, was, paradoxically, an unequivocal reminder of Jesus' divinity. Langmuir has pointed out that 'fifth and sixth century Christian artists depicted him as a classical nude in scenes of his Baptism in the River Jordan. They did so partly because he was then immersed in water, where he would have been expected to take off his clothes, but mainly because it was at the Baptism that his dual nature as man and God was revealed. The nudity once associated with Graeco-Roman statues of pagan gods, expressing ideal harmony and beauty, was still, at that date, the clearest visual sign of divinity.'[38]

It is all too easy to overlook that insight, and what Langmuir says of the baptism is equally true of the crucifixion. Jesus Himself saw his agony and death in 'baptismal' terms, as His challenge to His disciples in Matthew 20 'are ye able to drink of the cup that I shall drink of, and to be baptized with the baptism that I am baptized with? (v.22) makes clear. The voluntary laying aside of His clothing for His baptism by John in Jordan, and his forced stripping for His crucifixion, both reveal Him for who He is.

Another often overlooked convention in classical art also has a bearing on the subject; if, as Margaret Walters suggests,[39] 'the male . . . was taken as the norm and ideal,' then Beatrice Farwell's observation concerning this male body, that the 'most consistent of the idealisations is probably the device of representing the human body as entirely hairless', possibly, she suggests, because of 'the belief that hairiness was a sign of barbarism',[40] is equally normative. Here it is necessary to enter a caveat and draw a distinction between the depiction of the male and the female nude body, at least in classical statuary.

In respect of the male, the convention was that torso and limbs were depicted hairless, but that convention did not extend to the pubic area. In classical art, male genitalia and pubic hair are not hidden. As Farwell rather sarcastically remarked, 'the fig-leaf is biblical'.[41] By contrast, in the same period, the depiction of the female involved falsification; the *mons veneris* is shown both unified and hairless. At least, that is true in respect of what might be called 'public' sculpture and art; it is certainly not true of 'private' art, or erotica, as Martin Kilmer has shown conclusively.[42]

The details of the argument over the difference of depiction are both vexed and complex, and outside of the terms of reference of this paper. What is of importance is to keep in mind – though not uncritically – the fact that, as Emmanuel Cooper said, 'The perfect male form was considered the mirror of the soul . . . as close to sexual neutrality as the human body could achieve.'[43] Hugh Easton's figures of Christ, for example in the east window of St John's Church, Shirley, dating from 1949 – a figure repeated almost exactly six years later in St Martin's Church, Roath, Cardiff – can be said to exemplify the classical ideal; torso and limbs muscular, virile and hairless (even beardless, an artistic device Easton adopted from his mentor, Sir Ninian Comper) though for a 33-year-old middle-eastern Jew, perhaps impossibly blond-haired and youthful.[44]

It is this last point which, perhaps, makes it necessary to question Emmanuel Cooper's assertion that the classical male figure, nude – or, as in Easton's Christ as near nude as a prominently placed stained-glass window in a church would permit– is 'sexually neutral.'[45] Sir Kenneth (later Lord) Clark would not have agreed; in his *The Nude: A Study in ideal Form*,[46] he maintained that any nude in art that does not arouse in the viewer at least some slight quickening of sexual interest is 'bad art and false morals'. It is this honest assertion, cutting through as it does much pretentious and coy writing on the subject that confronts us with a truth, well expressed by Margaret Walters: 'the exposed body is emotionally charged and potentially subversive . . .':[47]

> The naked body can sum up everything we desire and everything we most fear. The body is the source of our deepest pleasures and traumas; our whole experience of the world is set by the way we experience our bodies . . . To see another person naked can reassure or alarm, satisfy curiosity or provoke guilt, arouse desire or disgust and often both together. The body preserves a memory of lost wholeness, and carries the seeds of our death.'[48]

In the light of that powerful statement, it is surely not possible to avoid the truth of Kenneth Clark's statement; not possible to regard Hugh

Easton's Christ figures in particular as 'sexually neutral.' Nor, arguably, did he intend them to be so regarded.

Bradley Smith is of some assistance here. 'It would seem', he wrote, 'that the creative impulse to paint [and, one could add, to sculpt] has often been stimulated by relating to the fundamental act of creation. Sex ... not reproduction, was the source, the model in one way or another ...'.[49] A work of art is both a creation and creative, and 'each viewer must ultimately judge for himself whether the artist has successfully transferred an experience to him.'[50] For some, the very idea that a 'religious' work of art might have any connection with sexuality or the sexual impulse verges on the sacrilegious or blasphemous'; for others it brings with it a sense of liberation, the breaking of an outmoded, but nonetheless still potent, taboo. For others again, and Leo Steinberg would be an excellent example, it is the re-affirmation of a neglected theological insight. As he put it: 'The Incarnate Word died as a full-fraught man, triumphant over both sin and death.'[51] It is His 'full-fraught' – that is, complete in every respect – humanity which is united with His divinity, humanity which does not in any way exclude sexuality. Thus Easton's *Christ in Glory* in St Martin's, Roath, Cardiff, bears the five wounds of His crucifixion on His fully human and fully sexual body into heaven.

It is necessary here not to wander into misunderstanding. As Steinberg says, 'naturalistic motifs in religious Renaissance art are never adequately accounted for by their prevalence in life situations'.[52] Thus when the person of Christ and 'sexuality' are juxtaposed, then this is done so for theological reasons. Again, as Steinberg asks, 'How could he who restores human nature to sinlessness be shamed by the sexual factor in his humanity?...Is this not reason enough to render Christ's sexual member ... like the stigmata, an object of *ostentation*?' This is a challenging notion; the definition of shame in traditional western Catholic teaching is 'the penalty of Original Sin' and in Christian belief in Christ, as the Epistle to the Hebrews asserts, 'we have not a high priest who cannot be touched with the feeling of our infirmities, but was in all points tempted as we are, yet without sin'.[53] Christ's exemplary virtue presupposes sexuality as a *sine qua non*; His chastity is not that of 'impotent abstinence, but in potency under check'.[54]

It is the contention of Steinberg that for the Renaissance artist there was nothing shameful – theologically speaking it was quite the opposite – in depicting the sexual potency of Christ, what he calls an '*ostentatio genitalium* comparable to the canonic *ostentation vulnerum*, the showing forth of the wounds'.[55] He gives for examples Maerten van Heemskerck's *Man of Sorrows* of *c*.1525, and Ludwig Krug's engraving of the same subject, of similar date. Steinberg shows that one way in which the *ostentation genitalium* was depicted was the showing of Christ in a state of tumescence, the erect male organ shrouded but made apparent by the folds of the loincloth. He asks the question that comes immediately to mind 'Are these works sacrilege or . . . affirmative Christian art?'[56] As an answer he proposes that such imagery is to be seen as a metaphor of 'the mortified-vivified flesh' of Christ. 'If the truth of the Incarnation was proved in the mortification of the penis, would not the truth of the Anastasis [resurrection] be proved by its erection? Would not this be the body's best show of power?'[57] This hypothesis overlooks the fact that the examples he gives, both the Krug and van Heemskerck artworks are of the Christ *before* His crucifixion and not *after* His resurrection, but it is, perhaps, rescued by reference to Titian's contemporary *Noli me Tangere*. In addition, as Xavier Bray has pointed out, 'the white garment that covers [Christ's] nakedness symbolically alludes to his resurrection'.[58] That selfsame garment appears in both the Krug and van Heemskerck artworks, and can be construed as a 'forward-reference' to the coming resurrection of the 'Man of Sorrows' who here awaits His crucifixion.

This discussion is not without its relevance to the study of the work of Hugh Easton and the search for the ideal male. Arguably, Easton's *Christ in Glory* in St Martin's, Roath, if the flowing drapery is carefully examined, makes the same allusion, and rather more obviously it may be found in the same figure in St John's, Shirley. It is most obvious of all in Easton's cartoon of 'Christ Ascending' at the V&A Archive.[59] In his response to Steinberg's thesis, the Jesuit Renaissance historian Fr John O'Malley asserted unequivocally that it fitted into the general tradition of Christian theology, 'but the immediate tradition of the religious culture of the Renaissance is even more confirmatory of his findings. The "dignity-of-man" theme, it seems to me, inspires, with a paradoxical bravado, the *ostentation genitalium*. . .'.[60] If, as it can be proposed, Hugh Easton shared in this Renaissance, dignity-of-man, vision, then his heroic, sexually dynamic, figures of the glorified Christ fit perfectly into Steinberg and O'Malley's conclusions about one aspect of that vision.

IV

It would, of course, be naive to believe that all unclothed figures in classical or Renaissance art, even those with explicitly 'religious' subject-matter are theologically orthodox and/or lacking in erotic charge. It is only necessary to think of the way in which the martyrdom of St Sebastian (a victim, it is believed, of the Diocletian persecution of Christians, sentenced to death by being shot with arrows) was depicted by artists from the sixteenth century onwards.[61] As Michael Jacobs put it, 'the subject of St Sebastian is the most notorious example of a sexually exploited religious subject . . . [the] possibilities [inherent] in the portrayal of a beautiful and defenceless body pierced by arrows . . .'.[62] It is not therefore surprising, perhaps, that certainly right up to recent times, St Sebastian became what has been called a 'gay icon'.

This introduces another strand in the search for the 'ideal male'; the necessity of taking into account the interest in the male body taken by the homosexual artist. As Jacobs says, 'although the nudes of, for example, Michelangelo have a spiritual intention, the artist was also physically attracted by the original models.'[63] The figures of Michelangelo's *David* of 1501–4 in Florence, of his *Risen Christ* of 1532–3 alluded to earlier, and of Donatello's *David* of nearly a century before, come immediately to mind. Walters said that 'the Renaissance was also a renaissance of homosexuality . . .',[64] and Florence was regarded at the time as an epicentre. Both Michelangelo and Donatello are believed to have been homosexual. Donatello's *David* is a celebration of adolescent beauty; the nudity and sexuality of Michelangelo's *David* is insistent.

The rather later artist, Caravaggio, is rather more overt; he dwells on details. In his *Amore Vincitore* of 1598–9 his Cupid poses provocatively, with one thigh raised as if he were climbing into bed, his penis prominent on the centre-line of the painting. As Walters says, 'the invitation could hardly be more direct'[65] – and the subject of the painting is a pre-pubescent boy. The same rather blatant sexuality is to be found in Caravaggio's *St John the Baptist*; the same overt display of the genitals, the same inviting grin, indeed, the same bed. If the message was not clear enough, this pre-pubescent John the Baptist is embracing a mature and well-horned ram, the epitome of male potency. It is worth recalling that at least one of Caravaggio's patrons, Cardinal Carlo Emanuele Pio de Carpi, who ended his days as Dean of the Sacred College, was suspected of paedophilia, and the *St John the Baptist* was in his art collection.

Certainly the depiction of John the Baptist as a pre-pubescent boy had a long lineage by the time of Caravaggio, as Domenico Veneziano's mid-fifteenth century painting shows. However, though Veneziano's child-John is naked, the figure is relaxed and unselfconscious. The same cannot be said of Caravaggio's John Baptist or his Cupid.

In this respect, two things have to be said about Hugh Easton's artwork. On the evidence it presents it can be argued that he was not immune from feelings of physical and possibly sexual attraction to his male subjects. In his *Seven Ages of Man* windows for the chapel of Oundle School, two figures in particular are notable in this respect. The windows are Easton's interpretation of Shakespeare's famous lines. His Soldier is one of his 'Brylcreem Boy' heroes, and his Lover a young, blond-haired man, alone among the set of figures not in contemporary dress, but clad in a loose, blouse-like shirt and tights, posed in an effeminate manner. Perhaps the best example of this kind of 'ideal male' is seen in the cartoon of a naked figure on horseback, which is not unlike what Margaret Walters called a 'newstand nude' which appeared in a 1974 issue of *Viva* magazine.[66] One is reminded again of the comment of one of Easton's father's correspondents that the artist necessarily protected his personal and private life, and kept 'many of his worlds' separate,[67] but his surviving papers, though arguably suggestive, do not provide evidence for the artist's homosexuality. (It needs to be borne in mind that the Sexual Offences Act, which decriminalised homosexual acts between consenting male adults over the age of 21 was not passed until 1967, nearly two years after Easton's death.)

Secondly, young male children do not figure prominently in his artwork. His Oundle 'Schoolboy' 'creeping unwillingly to school' is just that, a well-observed slouching figure. Children playing appear on a carved wooden plaque, one of the few examples of his work not in the medium of glass, with the Virgin Mary and the child Jesus,[68] but only in his cartoon for a window for Winchester Cathedral, inspired by Christ's first miracle at Cana in Galilee (John 2: 1–11),[69] and his figure of St John the Baptist at St Cybi's Church, Holyhead, is a naked or partially-clothed pre-pubescent or adolescent male figure met with. The prurience of Caravaggio is entirely absent; for Easton the male child or adolescent is the 'ideal male' *in potentia*.

How, then, to sum up this fascinating but elusive artist? 'Few things' said Edward Lucie-Smith, 'are more complex than our reactions to the naked or near-naked human body',[70] and the reaction to Easton's work is likely to be as complex and subjective as it is to the work of any artist. That he stood in the Classical and Renaissance tradition, with all that that implies, is probably indisputable; that he was fascinated by the male body is also beyond argument, but his reason or reasons for so being remain enigmatic. Unlike, for example, Michael Leonard in his *Stripped Torso* of 1980, he was not primarily exploring shapes, but recording character. Leonard drew from photographs,[71] and although Easton was certainly inspired by photographic images, as his scrapbook clearly shows, and his diaries give no evidence of sittings for models or their names (except in one case, and that of a woman, Susanna Fletcher, who is mentioned incidentally in a letter), the likelihood is that he did use models, in common with other artists like Rossetti and Edward Burne-Jones, who also designed for stained-glass. This does not preclude the possibility, even the probability, that Easton's 'ideal male', who appears again and again with minor variants, was a composite figure projected from his imagination.

Perhaps, in the end, the 'ideal male' has to be just that, for, as any search for the 'historical Jesus' is bound to be a fruitless quest, for every searcher has a subjective image of Him before setting out on the journey, so the search for the 'ideal male' is likely to be equally endless and fruitless. At least in Hugh Easton's case, there is a marvellous legacy of his search.

Notes

[1] The quotation continues: 'The dance may be mimetic, but it is the *verve* of the performance, not the closeness of the imitation, that impresses, and tame additions of truth will encumber and not convince. The dance must control the pantomime.' These words need to be borne in mind when seeking to understand the art of Hugh Easton. It is interesting that both this quote, and that from Balzac, appear at the beginning of Easton's scrapbook.

[2] Victoria & Albert Museum Archive of Art & Design [hereafter VAMAAD] 5/350/1983. Whoever was the author of the second quotation was familiar with Arthur Conan Doyle's Sherlock Holmes stories. An almost identical quotation appears in 'The Dancing Men'.

[3] For an introduction to Comper, see Anthony Symondson, *The Life and Work of Sir Ninian Comper 1864–1960, The Last Gothic Revivalist* (London, 1988).

[4] VAMAAD 5/365/1983. Dr Easton's Miscellaneous File. Letter of W I Croome of Barton Mill House, Cirencester, dated 3 October, 1965. Frederick Eden was another 'Old Wellingtonian', of an earlier generation, and he interceded for Hugh Easton with his father, convincing him of the rightness of his choice of career.

[5] Despite their personal abilities, after Easton's death in 1965 his assistants were unable to make the business viable, and the workshop soon closed.

6. VAMAAD 5/365/1983.
7. *Oxford Dictionary of National Biography* [hereafter ODNB].
8. *City of London Squadron Magazine*, 1965.
9. VAMAAD 5/365/1983. Letter dated 15 September, 1966.
10. VAMAAD 5/365/1983.
11. Ibid.
12. Ibid.
13. The little notebooks which he used as diaries had perforated margins, so it was easy for him (?) to remove pages without damaging the whole.
14. VAMAAD 5/350/1983. Wailes was sending Easton a copy of the Carthusian Rule.
15. They were almost exact contemporaries. Easton was born in 1906, and Fleming two years later. Fleming died in 1964, aged 56, having to all intents and purposes smoked and drunk himself to death, and Easton the following year, of what seems to have been bone cancer, aged 59. There is, however, no surviving evidence that the two knew one another.
16. Donald G. MacRae, *Weber* (London, 1974) p. 65.
17. Ibid., p. 12.
18. VAMAAD 5/317/1983.
19. To support this suggestion, his diaries often contain cryptic comments on the standard of the food he had been served.
20. VAMAAD 5/318/1983.
21. Michael Jacobs, *Nude Painting* (Oxford, 1979) p. 8.
22. Ibid., p. 9.
23. Beatrice Farwell, *Manet and the Nude. A Study in Iconography in the Second Empire* (New York, 1981) p. 29.
24. Margaret Walters, *The Nude Male. A New Perspective* (Harmondsworth, 1979) p. 7.
25. Mathieu Cocherau's 1814 painting 'Studio of David', now in the Louvre, Paris, is a good illustration of a life class with a nude male model.
26. Walters, op. cit., p. 37.
27. Michelangelo was, perhaps, the outstanding Renaissance inheritor and re-creator of this classical tradition. In addition to these works, see for example, his 'Dying Captive' of c.1514 (Louvre), 'Victory' of 1527–30 (Florence, Palazzo Vecchio) and figures in the Sistine Chapel in Rome.
28. VAMAAD 5/350/1983.
29. So called from the popular male hair-cream of the time.
30. Quoted on *http://www.rolls-royce.com/history/overview/memorial.jsp* (accessed 20 March 2008).
31. The constraints of a single paper will not permit any analysis of these sanctified warriors. Easton's place in the study of militarism and the military metaphor in stained-glass art deserves a separate paper.
32. John O'Malley, SJ, Postscript to Leo Steinberg, *The Sexuality of Christ in Renaissance Art and in Modern Oblivion* (London, 1983) p. 200.
33. Ibid.
34. The art historian Kenneth Clark drew a distinction between 'naked' and 'nude' (*The Nude: A Study of Ideal Art*, London, 1956, p. 3), the latter being defined by him as 'an art form invented by the Greeks in the fifth century BC'. As Beatrice Farwell observed, op. cit., p. 4, Clark thus created what she considered to be a false distinction between the 'naked', i.e. an unclothed figure of reality, and the 'nude', a classical ideal. This denied to the former any status in art. Unless one sticks to English, the distinction tends to disappear in other

languages. It is in any case not helpful, and reveals a rather fastidious distaste for the 'real' in art as opposed to the depiction of the 'ideal'. This is an on-going debate, which shows few signs of ending.

35   Not just one, as Erika Langmuir maintains in her essay 'The Saving Body' in Gabriele Finaldi (ed.), *The Image of Christ* (London and New Haven, 2000) p. 169.
36   See for example Gill's 1918 pencil drawing of the crucified Christ; another Crucifixion of 1922; and his torso sculpture of the same year, 'Deposition', now at King's School, Canterbury. Malcolm Yorke, *Eric Gill. Man of Flesh and Spirit* (London, 1981).
37   Quoted by Yorke, op. cit., p. 43.
38   Finaldi, op. cit., p. 169.
39   Walters, op. cit., p. 7.
40   Farwell, op. cit., p. 31.
41   Ibid. The reference is to Genesis 3: 7. The coy addition of the 'fig-leaf' owes more to prudery than it does to art.
42   Martin F. Kilmer, *Greek Erotica on Attic Red-Figure Vases* (London, 1993), especially pp. 133–59. See also Ove Brusendorff and Poul Henningsen, *A History of Eroticism. Antiquity* (New York, 1963). Kilmer effectively disposes of the argument that the female pudenda were so depicted because they were normally shaven at this date.
43   Emmanuel Cooper, *The Sexual Perspective. Homosexuality and Art in the last Hundred Years in the West* (London, 2nd edn 1994), p. 1.
44   Easton's window is high in the 'liturgical east' wall of the church, above and behind the High Altar. The overall design is subtle as well as arresting; the figure of Christ is set in plain glass, so the changing colours of the sky beyond, the movement of clouds, behind the glowing figure presents the worshipper facing it from the body of the church with a kaleidoscopic effect which is endlessly fascinating. John R. Guy, 'The Art and Architecture of the Catholic Revival in Roath', *Roath Local History Society Project newsletter*, 6, no. 2, 1991, pp. 30–57, at p. 40. Also John R. Guy, *A History of Roath St Martin* (unpublished typescript, 1962), pp. 49–50. Easton also designed another window for the church, in the Holy Cross Chapel, to replace one destroyed in the blitz of 1941. It depicts the Cross, in green glass, with the consecrated Eucharistic elements at its centre. As with the original, it is a memorial to the Revd Harry North, Priest-in-charge of the church from 1889–97.
45   Although there are a number of subjects from the Old and New Testament narratives which have enabled artists to include naked figures in their compositions, e.g. David and Bathsheba, Susannah and the Elders, come immediately to mind, none are, perhaps for obvious contextual reasons, suitable for stained-glass. The one exception would be the pre-lapsarian Adam and Eve, and even this subject has not been a common choice for stained-glass artists and their patrons. Hugh Easton designed one window with this subject (VAMAAD AAD/1983/5/21) for Durham Cathedral. However, the window was not intended for a worship-space, but for the Chapter House.
46   London, 1960, p. 29.
47   Walters, op. cit., p. 11.
48   Ibid., p. 10.
49   Bradley Smith, *Erotic Art of the Masters. The 18th, 19th and 20th Centuries* (New York, n.d.) p. viii.
50   Ibid., p. 108.
51   Steinberg, op. cit., unpaginated, but associated with Fig. 122.
52   Ibid., p. 8.
53   Hebrews 4: 15.

54 Steinberg, op. cit., p. 17.
55 Ibid., p. 1.
56 Ibid., p. 86.
57 Ibid., p. 91.
58 Finaldi, op.cit., p. 172.
59 VAMAAD AAD/1983/5/23.
60 Steinberg, op. cit., p. 201.
61 This early version of the 'firing squad' was unsuccessful. According to the traditional story, Sebastian survived, and his wounds were tended and healed by the widow of another martyr, St Castulus. On hearing this, the emperor then ordered that Sebastian be battered to death.
62 Jacobs, op. cit., pp. 34–5.
63 Ibid., p. 34.
64 Walters, op. cit., p. 111.
65 Ibid., p. 188.
66 VAMAAD AAD/5/20/1983. 'Newstand Nude' is the heading of chapter 10 of Walters' work, op. cit.
67 VAMAAD AAD 5/365/1983.
68 VAMAAD AAD 1983/5/141.
69 VAMAAD AAD 5/10/2/1983.
70 Edward Lucie-Smith, *The Body. Images of the Nude* (London, 1981) p. 7.
71 Ibid., p. 163.

THE WORKS OF JOHN MORGAN-GUY

1961
(with Roger Wools) *The Parish Church of St Mary the Virgin, Caerau* (8 pp.).

1963
'Churches of the Vale' (series of 27 articles, *South Wales Echo*).

1964
Churches of Cardiff (series of 27 articles, *South Wales Echo*).
'The Old Bishop's Palace, Llandaff', *Province*, 15, no. 3, pp. 96–101.

1965
'The medieval Vale of Glamorgan in 1965', *Province*, 16, no. 1, pp. 33–6.
'William Edward Boys, priest, 1874–1955', *Province*, 16, no. 3, pp. 96–102.
'Flintstones and Death in Bronze; the Pant-y-Maen Hoard', *Gateway*, NS, 19, pp. 4–5.

1966
'Some ecclesiastical peculiarities of south Glamorgan, human and otherwise', *Province*, 17, no. 3, pp. 83–7.

1968
'Excavations in the Old Bishop's Palace, Llandaff 1962–1963', *Province*, 19, no. 1, pp. 11–13.
'Llandough – Our History' (series of 12 articles), *Llandough & Leckwith Magazine*.

1969
'Roath Confessional', *Impact*, pp. 17–20.

1970

'The Gamage Family; a study in clerical patronage in the 17th and 18th centuries', *Morgannwg*, 14, pp. 35-61.

'Why keep these treasures hidden?' (article for Conservation Year), *South Wales Echo*, 12 October.

'The chapel of St Thomas the Martyr in Cardiff. St Mary's', *Cardiff Magazine*, November, pp. 6-7 and 11-12.

'The P'she Church Callyd Saynete Maris', *A History & Description of the Mother Church of Cardiff* (48 pp.).

1973

'The Reverend John Carne of Nash', *Journal of the Historical Society of the Church in Wales*, 23, pp. 56-70.

1974

'The Church in Cardiff', *The Cardiff Book*, 2, ed. Stewart Williams, pp. 154-71.

1976

'William Beaw: Bishop and Secret Agent', *History Today*, 26, no. 12, pp. 796-803.

1977

'Medieval Chapels of the town and castle of Caerphilly', *Caerphilly, The Journal of the Caerphilly Local History Society*, 4, pp. 22-4.

'Bishop Richard Watson and his Lakeland friends', *Transactions of the Cumberland & Westmorland Antiquarian & Archaeological Society*, 77, pp. 139-44.

1978-9

'The Prebends of Llandaff Cathedral (series of 14 articles), *Llandaff Monthly*.

1979

'Perpetual Curacies in Eighteenth Century South Wales', *Studies in Church History*, 16, ed. Derek Baker, pp. 327-33.

'1829-1979, A brief history of The Devauden Chapel through 150 years' (30 pp.)

(with Ewart B. Smith) *Ancient Gwent Churches* (72 pp.).

1980
(with Ewart B. Smith) *Ancient Gwent Churches* (72 pp.), reprint of 1979.

1981
'Church and Churchmen in Llantrisant Parish, 1660–1800', *Glamorgan Historian*, 12, ed. Roy Denning, pp. 81–92.
'The Anglican Patronage of Monmouthshire Recusants in the Seventeenth & Eighteenth Centuries: some examples', *Recusant History*, 15, no. 6, pp. 452–4.
'Bishop Barrington's Book', *Morgannwg*, 25, pp. 112–29.

1982
Milton Clevedon Church in Somerset (80 pp.).
'Eighteenth Century Gwent Catholicism', *Recusant History*, 16, no. 1, pp. 78–88.
'The significance of indigenous clergy in the Welsh Church at the Restoration', *Studies in Church History*, 18, ed. Stewart Mews, pp. 335–43.
'Kilgwrrwg Church', *Gwent Local History*, 53, pp. 38–45.
'Archbishop Secker as a Physician', *Studies in Church History*, 19, ed. W. J. Sheils, pp. 127–135.
'Wells Cathedral from the Reformation to 1800', *Wells Cathedral – A History*, ed. L. S. Colchester, pp. 148–78.
'The episcopal licensing of physicians, surgeons and midwives', *Bulletin of the History of Medicine*, 56, pp. 528–42.

1983
'Hospitals and Infirmaries. Leeches and Lancets', Guide/Catalogue of the Exhibition of Medical Treatment 1750–1850, Bath, Camden Works Museum, 5 August–16 September, pp. 12–13.
'De Medicina Statica: Archbishop Thomas Secker, A Forgotten English Iatromechanist', *Histoire des Sciences Medicales*, Tome XVII, Numero Special/2, pp. 134–7.
Y.D.H. 1858–1983. The Story of Yeovil District Hospital in pictures (73 pp.).
'Under the Dean's Nose. Recusancy in early Seventeenth Century Wells', *South Western Catholic History*, 1, pp. 10–18.

1984

'An Investigation into the Pattern and Nature of Patronage, Plurality and Non-Residence in the old diocese of Llandaff between 1660 and the beginning of the Nineteenth Century', University of Wales Ph.D. thesis (2 vols, 864 pp.).

'Doctor's Recipe Book? (possible identification of a 17th century Bath Abbey MS as the compilation of Dr Robert Pierce)', *Pharmaceutical Historian*, 14, no. 1, pp. 6–8.

Mr Bird and his Infirmary. Crewkerne Hospital 1866–1904, 1984 (50 pp.).

'Surgeons and Surgery in Nineteenth Century Yeovil', *Bristol Medico-Chirurgical Journal*, 99 (ii), 370, pp. 48–50.

'Good Practices in Mental Health in Yeovil and District', An International Hospital Federation Project (60 pp.).

'Saving Flat Holm's Cholera Hospital', *Exploring Local History*, 8, pp. 244–7.

'Flat Holm's Isolation Hospital 1884–1937', *Search: Journal of the Banwell Society of Archaeology*, 20, pp. 65–79 (reprinted text of the paper in *Exploring Local History*, with further illustrations).

1985

'Medical Books at Wells Cathedral', Catalogue compiled for a visit by the Royal Society of Medicine Section of the History of Medicine (unpaginated).

'Would a Regional Liaison Body be Helpful? The Continuing Saga of Medical Records', Report for the Society of Archivists, pp. 59–63.

(with Anne Hargreaves) 'William Alfred Hunt (1845–1929): Local Anaesthetic Pioneer', *British Dental Journal*, 159, no. 6, pp. 193–4.

1986

'Some Medical Clerics of Wells Cathedral', *The Friends of Wells Cathedral Report*, pp. 18–20.

'Every Morning New Horizons, Every Night New Stars. The contribution of William Alfred Hunt to Anaesthesia', *Anaesthesia Points West*, 19, no. 2, pp. 48–50.

Malachi's Monument. The Taunton & Somerset Hospital at East Reach (110 pp.).

1987

(with Betty Burbage), *Pubs Ancient & Modern in Crewkerne* (24 pp.).

'Richard Watson and the role of a bishop', *Bibliotheque de la Revue d'Histoire Ecclesiastique*, fasc.72, pp. 390-7.
(with Jean M. Guy), 'A.I.D.S. & the Churchman', *Hendford Herald*, 2, pp. 3-4.
'The day the chaplains were sacked', *Hendford Herald*, 5, pp. 1-2.

1988

Exhibition Catalogue of Medical Books in Wells Cathedral Library, for the Third World Congress on Prison Health Care (8 pp.).
'Hulk and Holm: England's Offshore Battle against Cholera', *Verfahren Internationaler Kongress fur Geschichte der Medizin, Dusseldorf*, pp. 833-7.
'The Greatest of Whips and the Least of Theologians. The Revd Lord William Somerset 1784-1851', *Journal of Welsh Ecclesiastical History*, 5, pp. 81-95.

1989

'The Empoisoned Darts of Venus: John Warren, MD, A Pioneer West Country Venereologist', *Bristol Medico-Chirurgical Journal*, 104 (i), pp. 17-18.
'Fishing for the Soul "Nor'ard of the Dogger"', *Studies in Church History*, pp. 415-22.
'Immoderate Toil and other Causes: Disease, Death and Yeovil Glovers in the mid-Nineteenth Century', *Chronicle, the Journal of Yeovil Archaeological and Local History Society*, 4, 4, pp. 108-21.

1990

'The Shadow of the Fever Van', *A Pox on the Provinces!* (ed. Roger Rolls, Jean M. Guy and John R. Guy), pp. 39-49.

1991

'The Welsh Connection: Roman Catholicism in Somerset and South Wales in the Eighteenth and early Nineteenth Centuries', *South Western Catholic History*, 9, pp. 3-10.
'The Art and Architecture of the Catholic Revival in Roath', *Roath Local History Society*, 6, no. 2, pp. 30-57.
'Archbishop Thomas Secker and "The duties of the sick"', *Actes du XXXIIe Congres International d'Histoire de la Medecine*, Antwerp, pp. 139-44.

'Ten Years at Trinity', *Sermons and Addresses* (236 pp.).
The Diocese of Llandaff in 1763. The Primary Visitation of Bishop Ewer, South Wales Record Society (212 pp.).
'Bishop Watkin Williams and "the Lambeth Farce"', *Journal of Welsh Ecclesiastical History*, 8, pp. 55–9.
'Ahoy! Patient Coming Aboard: Floating Hospitals for Infectious Diseases', *Medical Sciences Historical Society*, 10, pp. 11–22.

1991–3
'What did they die of?' (series of five articles), *The Greenwood Tree*, Somerset and Dorset Family History Society, vols 16, no. 4; 17, nos 1, 2, 4; 18, no. 1.

1992
The Chapel in the Tithing. St Mary the Virgin, Chesterblade (30 pp.).

1993
'The Port of Tyne Sanitary Authority: Floating Hospitals, beri-beri and bubonic plague. Medicine in Northumbria', *Essays on the History of Medicine in the North–East of England*, ed. David Gardner-Medwin et al., pp. 286–300.

1994
'Compassion and the art of the possible. Dr Southwood Smith as a social reformer and public health pioneer', Octavia Hill Memorial Lecture (18 pp.).
'Wales, the Baltic Trade and Cholera in the late nineteenth century. Russia and Wales', *Essays on the History of State Involvement in Health Care*, ed. John H. Cule and John M. Lancaster, pp. 87–100.

1995
Milton Clevedon Church in Somerset, (2nd edition; first published 1982 (53 pp.).
'Flat Holm Isolation Hospital 1884–1937', *Flat Holm Bristol Channel Island*, ed. Bob Jory et al., pp. 84–97 (reprint of the paper published in *Search*, 1984).
'The Rudry Radical. Dr William Price of Ty'nycoedcae' (Part 1), *Caerphilly: the Journal of the Caerphilly Local History Society*, 5, pp. 28–35.
The Life of Bettws School 1896–1995 (56 pp.).

1996
St Mary's Church, Llanllugan. A Brief History (9 pp.).

1997
Entries in *The Oxford Dictionary of the Christian Church*, ed. B. Livingstone.
Entries in *The Oxford Companion to British History*, ed. John Cannon.

1998
'Thomas Mills Hoare. An Eighteenth Century Vicar of St Woolos. His Life as a reflection of his Times', *Friends of St Woolos' Cathedral Annual Report*, pp. 5–20.

1999
(ed. with Kathryn Jenkins and Frances Knight) *Wales, Women and Religion in Historical Perspective.*
'Riding against the Clock. The Visitations of Edward Tenison in Carmarthen and Ossory in the early Eighteenth Century, *Contrasts and Comparisons: Studies in Irish and Welsh Church History*, ed. John R. Guy and W. G. Neely, pp. 55–64.

2000
'The Society of St David. Some reflections on its History', *Verbum. The Termly Magazine of the Chapel of St David's College, Lampeter* (unpaginated).
'The Rudry Radical. Dr William Price of Ty'nycoedcae (Part 2)', *Caerphilly, the Journal of the Caerphilly Local History Society*, pp. 52–64.

2002
'From the Coral Strand to the Dulas Brook. Thomas Phillips, 1760–1851', *A Bold Imagining. University of Wales, Lampeter. Glimpses of an unfolding vision*, ed. Keith Robbins and John Morgan-Guy, with Wyn Thomas, pp. 37–40.
What did the poets see? A Theological and Philosophical Reflection.

2003
(with Peter Lord), *The Visual Culture of Wales. Medieval Vision* (288 pp.).

2004

'Close Action off The Coromandel Coast: A Founders' Library Manuscript and the British Fight for India' *Readers, Printers, Churchmen, and Travellers: Essays in Honour of David Selwyn*, ed. William Marx and Janet Burton, *Trivium*, 35, pp. 97–120.

2005

(with Madeleine Grey) '"A better and frugal life". Llanllugan and Cistercian Women's Houses in Wales', *Archaeologia Cambrensis*, 154, pp. 97–114.

'The Margam Concordantiae: Mystical Theology and a Twelfth Century Cistercian Community in Wales', *Morgannwg*, XLIX, pp. 9–33.

Entries in *Celtic Culture: An Historical Encyclopaedia* (5 vols), ed. John T. Koch.

2006

'The Man who Isn't There (But Nearly Always Was)', *Acorn. Journal of the Octavia Hill Society*, 3, 2005–6, pp. 97–127.

'Revolutionary End to a Chaplaincy', *The European Anglican*, no. 31, p. 16.

2007

'The Use of the Dead to the Living. Jeremy Bentham, Thomas Southwood Smith, Happiness and Dissection', *The Nature and Culture of the Human Body*, ed. Peter Mitchell, *Trivium*, 37, pp. 45–64.

'Shrine and Counter-Shrine in 1920s and 1930s Dewisland', *St David of Wales. Cult, Church and Nation*, ed. J. Wyn Evans and Jonathan M. Wooding, pp. 286–95.

2008

'"A Cultivated and Well-Stored Mind". Thomas Phillips, MRCS, Benefactor of St David's College, Lampeter', *The Link*, LXI, pp. 5–6.

'John Henry Filmer, Priest, 1869–1959', *The Ransomer*, XXXVI, no. 5, pp. 11–19.

'John Henry Filmer, Priest, 1869–1959', *The Beda Review*, pp. 29–36 (reprinted from *The Ransomer*).

'Public Space and Private Prayer: the church building as *locus* for personal devotion. The Welsh Medieval Church and its Context', On-line Conference Proceedings (unpaginated).

'Imaging the Bible. Two Contrasting Works in Carmarthenshire Churches', *Carmarthenshire Life*, pp. 18–19.

'Sermons in Glass. Fishguard's Stained-Glass Windows', *Pembrokeshire Life*, pp. 4–5.

'The Bible and Medieval Art', *Imaging the Bible. An Introduction to Biblical Art*, ed. Martin O'Kane, pp. 41–62.

2009

'Fiery Angels and Country Parsons', *Imaging the Bible in Wales*. Icon News, 20, pp. 18–22.

'"Tinkers and other Vermin". Methodism and the Established Church in Wales 1735–1800', *Revival, Renewal and the Holy Spirit*, ed. Dyfed Wyn Roberts, pp. 27–35.

(with Daveth H. Frost), 'The Medieval Church and Society', *Saving St Teilo's. Bringing a medieval church to life*, ed. Gerallt Nash, pp. 20–1.

'Arthur, Harri Tudor and the Iconography of Loyalty in Wales', *Arthur Tudor, Prince of Wales. Life, Death and Commemoration*, ed. Steven Gunn and Linda Monckton, pp. 50–63.

'Religion and Belief, 1660–1780', *Gwent County History*, vol. 3, ed. Madeleine Grey and Prys Morgan, pp. 146–73.

2010

'"A Cultivated and Well-Stored Mind". Thomas Phillips, MRCS', An Introductory Essay, Exhibition Catalogue: *Thomas Phillips and the Greatest Little Library in Wales* (unpaginated).

'"A Cultivated and Well-Stored Mind". Thomas Phillips, MRCS', *Cronicl Powys*, Powys Family History Society, 81, pp. 22–4 (reprinted from The Link and the Exhibition Catalogue).

'Biblical Art from Wales. Setting the Scene', *Biblical Art from Wales*, ed. Martin O'Kane and John Morgan-Guy, pp. 11–44.

2011

(with Peter Lord) 'Visual Culture', *Gwent County History*, vol. 4, ed. Chris Williams and Sian Rhiannon Williams, pp. 252–64.

'The Oxford Movement and its Effect in Wales', *Welsh Journal of Religious History*, 6, pp. 49–68.

2012
'Sermons in Wales in the Established Church', *The Oxford Handbook to the British Sermon 1689-1901*, ed. Keith A. Francis, William Gibson, Robert Ellison, John Morgan-Guy and Bob Tennant, pp. 183-98.

2013
(with Peter Lord), 'Visual Culture', *Gwent County History*, vol. 5, ed. Chris Williams and Andy Croll, pp. 274-82.

'Trials and Shadows. Bishop Charles John Ellicott 1819-1905 and "angry controversies" in the Church of England', *Religion, Identity and Conflict in Britain from the Restoration to the Twentieth Century*, ed. Stewart J. Brown, Frances Knight and John Morgan-Guy, pp. 137-56.

'The Red Flag and a pair of Scissors. An Anglican Chaplaincy and the 1917 Russian Revolution', *Welsh Journal of Religious History*, 7 and 8, pp. 154-70.

2014
'The Church in Wales', 'The Moravian Church', 'The Religious History of Wales', *Religious Life and Practice in Wales from the Seventeenth Century to the Present Day*. Ed. Richard C. Allen and David Ceri Jones, with Trystan O. Hughes (Cardiff, Welsh Academic Press) pp. 13-26, 107-13.

'Cardiff and the Bubonic Plague, 1900-1901', *Morgannwg*, LVIII, pp. 5-18.

2015
'The Diocese of St Davids in the Reformation Era 1: From Rebellion to Reaction 1485-1553', 'The Diocese of St Davids in the Reformation Era II: From Reaction to Restoration 1553-1660', *Religion and Society in the Diocese of St Davids 1485-2011*, ed. William Gibson and John Morgan-Guy (Farnham, Ashgate) pp. 13-36, 37-62.

2016
'The Visit of the Eastern Metropolitans and Patriarchs to St Davids Cathedral in 1925', *Friends of St Davids Cathedral Annual Report for 2015*, pp. 12-19.

'Rowland Williams (1817–1870), 150', *Lampeter. The Birthplace of Welsh Rugby*, Exhibition Catalogue, Roderic Bowen Library and Archives, for the commemoration of the 150th anniversary of the game of rugby in Wales.

2017

'A Day in the Life of East Reach Hospital. 19th February 1850', *West of England Medical Journal*, 116, no. 3, unpaginated; on-line publication.

2018

'Thomas Secker, M.D.: Archbishop and man-midwife', *Journal of Medical Biography*, 2, pp. 102–10.
'Bog-Oak, Rubstones and the Sheffield Warming Company. Tregynon Church and the Victorian Gothic Revival', *Montgomeryshire Collections*, 106, pp. 117–26.
'The Reverend Austin Oakley: An Anglican Priest who became a Respected Friend of the Orthodox Church', *Sobornost*, 39, 2, pp. 71–85.
'"Petals on a Wet, Black Bough": The Established Church, Methodism and Dissent in the Diocese of Llandaff in 1763', *Wesley and Methodist Studies*, 20, 2, pp. 132–50.
'"The person appointed must be prepared to go at once": SPG Chaplains in the Crimean War', *Royal Army Chaplains' Department Journal*, 56, pp. 86–95.
'*The Rich Man in His Castle. The Life, Family and Ministry of the Reverend Wentworth Watson, 1848–1925*', The Anglo-Catholic History Society, 35 pp., illus.
'The College Afloat: St David's College Alumni Serving on Board Ship during World War 1' (Lampeter, UWTSD Roderic Bowen Library and Archives, Exhibition; accompanying lecture), 23 pp., illus. (also printed in Welsh as *Y Coleg ar y Môr: Cyn-fyfyrwyr Coleg Dewi Sant a fu'n Gwasanaethu ar Longau yn ystod y Rhyfel Byd 1af*).
'The Restoration Episcopate in the diocese of Llandaff, and new light on that of Bishop William Lloyd', *Morgannwg*, LXII, pp. 48–77.

2019

'The Visit of the Eastern Metropolitans and Patriarchs to St Davids Cathedral in 1925. From the East to the Isles', *Approaches to the Eastern Connections of the Early Churches of Britain and Ireland*, ed. Jonathan M. Wooding and Andrew Louth (Oxford, Fellowship of St Alban and St Sergius) pp. 112–29, illus.

'The Derry Ormond Tower and the Battle of Waterlo' (Lampeter, UWTSD Roderic Bowen Library and Archives, Exhibition; accompanying essay), 9 pp., illus. (also printed in Welsh as 'Tŵr y Dderi a Brwydr Waterloo').

'The College, Hitler's Deputy, and Churchill's Secret Army' (Lampeter, UWTSD Roderic Bowen Library and Archives, Exhibition; accompanying essay), 6 pp., illus. (also printed in Welsh as 'Y Coleg, Dirprwy Hitler, a Byddin Gêl Churchill').

'Henry James Prince. The Lampeter Student who believed he was God' (Lampeter, UWTSD Roderic Bowen Library and Archives, Exhibition; accompanying essay), 9 pp., illus. (also printed in Welsh as 'Henry James Prince. Y Myfyriwr o Lambed a Gredai ei fod yn Dduw').

'"Receiving scorn and mocking": the iconography of the *Christ aux outrages* in Wales and the Western European tradition', *Archaeologia Cambrensis*, 168, pp. 229–43, illus.

'Morgan Rhys (1716–1779) of Cil-y-cwm. Schoolmaster, Preacher and Hymnwriter' (Lampeter, UWTSD Roderic Bowen Library and Archives, Exhibition; accompanying essay), 6 pp., illus (also printed in Welsh as 'Morgan Rhys (1716–1779) o Gil-y-cwm. Athro, Pregethwr ac Emynydd').

'Cardiganshire in the Era of the Reformation', *Cardiganshire County History. Volume 2. Medieval and Early Modern Cardiganshire*, ed. Geraint H. Jenkins, Richard Suggett and Eryn M. White (Cardiff, University of Wales Press), pp. 453–80.

'Lampeter and the Atom Bomb' (Lampeter, UWTSD Roderic Bowen Library and Archives, Exhibition; accompanying essay), 6 pp., illus. (also printed in Welsh as 'Llambed a'r Bom Atomig').

'The Corpse as a Commodity. The College Treasurer's Family and the Body Snatchers' (Lampeter, UWTSD Roderic Bowen Library and Archives, Exhibition; accompanying essay), 10 pp., illus. (also printed in Welsh as 'Y Corff fel Nwydd. Teulu Trysorydd y Coleg a'r Cipwyr Cyrff').

'Forgotten People in Hidden Places' (series of twelve monthly short essays on the website of The Friends of Friendless Churches, to coincide with the Welsh Tourist Board's 2020 Visit Wales – Year of Discovery.

2020

'The Professor, His Aunt (and a Dog) Go Climbing', (Lampeter, UWTSD Roderic Bowen Library and Archives, Exhibition; accompanying essay), 10 pp., illus. (also printed in Welsh as 'Yr Athro, Ei Fodryb (a'i Gi) yn Mynd i Ddringo').

'Lemuel J. Hopkin James (1874–1937) "A gruff, but kindly, little Welshman"', and 'William J. C. Lindsay (1832–1912), Aristocratic Welsh Priest', in Michael Yelton (ed.), *Twenty Priests for Twenty Years. A Commemorative Volume to mark the Twentieth Anniversary of the Anglo-Catholic History Society* (London, Anglo-Catholic History Society), pp. 87–97 and 169–179, illus.

'Separated by Open Water: Pluralism across the Bristol Channel in the Eighteenth Century', *Morgannwg*, LXIII, pp. 32–49.

'Abergavenny Priory, The "Lost" Annals, and a Piers Plowman Manuscript', *The Monmouthshire Antiquary*, XXXV, pp. 37–47.

ISBN 978-1-78683-809-4
eISBN 978-1-78683-810-0
ISSN (Print) 2057-4517
ISSN (Online) 2057-4525
The Journal of Religious History, Literature and Culture
© University of Wales Press, 2021
Articles and reviews © The Contributors, 2021

Printed by CPI Group (UK) Ltd

Contributors to The Journal of Religious History, Literature and Culture should refer enquiries to the journal page at www.uwp.co.uk or e-mail press@press.wales.ac.uk requesting notes for contributors.

Advertising enquiries should be sent to the Sales and Marketing Department at the University of Wales Press, at the address below.

Subscriptions: The Journal of Religious History, Literature and Culture is published twice a year in June and November. The annual subscription for institutions is £95 (print only), £85 (online only) or £140 (combined); and for individuals is £25 (print or online only) or £40 (combined). Subscription orders should be sent to University of Wales Press, University Registry, King Edward VII Avenue, Cardiff CF10 3NS. E-mail: press@press.wales.ac.uk.

Open Access: The University of Wales Press (UWP) is fully committed to the principle of Open Access for those authors requiring it, whether by funder mandate, REF or otherwise. It is incumbent on contributors to state clearly if they have an Open Access requirement when submitting an article.

UWP's policy is to require an embargo period of eighteen months for Green Open Access, to begin on the last day in the month of publication of the print version. We also welcome submissions for Gold Open Access: if required, please contact the Commissioning Department at UWP to discuss an Article Processing Charge (APC) for your article.

The version of record for deposit should be the author's accepted and final peer-reviewed text, for non-commercial purposes.

The inclusion of third-party material in the deposited article will be at the author/institution's own risk. Authors should continue to ensure clearance of rights for third-party material for print and e-publication in the usual way for the purposes of the version published by UWP and for Open Access, if your article is Open Access.

UWP will continue to accept and publish articles by authors without requirements for REF under pre-existing arrangements.

For more information on our current Open Access policy, please visit our website: *www.uwp.co.uk/open-access.*